I0542828

Wisdom from a Life in Minstry

Bob Plunket

Compiled by
Rickey Collum

Copyright © 2023 by Bob Plunket

Published by Cypress Publications

Manufactured in the United States of America

Cataloging-in-Publication Data

Plunket, Bob

Wisdom from a life in ministry

p. cm.

ISBN 978-1-956811-51-3(pbk.) 978-1-956811-52-9 (ebook)

1. Devotional literature. 2. Inspiration. 3. Christian life—Churches of
Christ author. I. Author. II. Collum, Rickey, editor. III. Title.

242.2—dc20

LLibrary of Congress Control Number: 2023944863

Cover design by Brittany Vander Maas.
All rights reserved. No part of this publication may be reproduced,
distributed, stored in a retrieval system, or transmitted in any form or by any
means without the prior written permission of the publisher, except in the
case of brief quotations embodied in critical reviews and certain other
noncommercial uses permitted by copyright law.

Cypress Publications
3625 Helton Drive
PO Box HCU
Florence, AL 35630

www.hcu.edu

Note from the Compiler

I would be remiss if I did not include a few acknowledgments and special thanks to Bob Plunket and his family for allowing me to compile this book. Also, thanks to my helpers, Linda Raper, Carolyn Braden, Jean Black, Nancy Frederick, Wanda Lawler, and Kathy McCarley, without your help and insight this book would not have been published. As in all things, I give thanks to God and my loving wife, Lisa.

Rickey Collum

Contents

Introduction

As a preacher and a member of the church of Christ, I think we fail to realize how prevalent the brotherhood is in northern Alabama. In our little corner of the world, we are blessed to have between 70-80 churches.

When one thinks about this unprecedented number of congregations in such a small area, the question arises, how did this happen? Most people go back to the beginning of Mars Hill Bible College started in 1871, by T. B. Larimore. That could be the answer, but how have those churches survived for over 150 years? The answer I believe is good solid biblical preaching. That school produced giants in the brotherhood, such as F. D. Srygley and J. C. McQuiddy, both notable restoration preachers. From that small beginning, this area has enjoyed good preachers, and it is because of those men of God that we are still blessed.

As a member of the church of Christ, I believe we should all pay tribute to the preachers and elders on whose shoulders we stand today. This was how the first book I compiled came about. Ted Burleson and I discovered a large box of notes and articles about the Holy Spirit, that had been put together by Jack Wilhelm, a well-known preacher in our area. From that box, we edited the book, *A Study of the Holy Spirit* (Cypress Publications, 2021).

You would think that would never happen again, but while preaching at the Hackleburg Church of Christ, a deacon, Freddie Poe came to me asking for a book of sermons written by Bob Plunket. He explained that Mr. Plunket and he had bird hunted together for many years, and he had heard there was a book of Brother Plunket's sermons. Bob Plunket and his brother, Lamar, were well-known preachers in the area since the 1960s. Bob has preached for 70 years; 33 of those years were at Tuscumbia Church of Christ, 10 at Sherrod Avenue Church of Christ, and ended his preaching career at Colbert Heights Church of Christ. I knew one of Brother Plunket's daughters from Mars Hill Bible School and contacted her about the book. She explained that there was a book put together for the family years ago, but it was not a book of sermons.

From that encounter, Freddie and I were invited to Brother Plunket's house in Tuscumbia, Alabama. We meet a man of 92 years, who, except for a problem with his leg, was in good health. We sat and after the introductions, we were shown his lovely home in which almost every room pictures were displayed of Jan, his beautiful wife of 66 years. His love for her was as evident as his sorrow for her passing in 2018. It was good to hear these good men speak of tales of bird hunting and to see their friendship rekindle.

Much to my surprise the subject changed — could I could help bring about a book of his sermons, sadly most of his sermons were on cassette tape, which would make the editing extremely difficult. Luckily, we were brought a huge

Introduction

box of bulletin articles going back 40-50 years. Looking at these articles, I could see the excellent work and thought that went into the preparation of each one. I began to see the book unfold; by carefully choosing these articles, the reader could see the history and the work of a fine preacher. Young preachers could use these today as sermon starters. The ideas of that day have turned into the book in your hand, I hope you enjoy getting to know Bob Plunket as much as I have.

Rickey Collum

Wisdom from a Life in Minstry

Scent or Sight?

THE GREYHOUND HUNTS BY SIGHT. HE IS FAST, streamlined, and beautiful. He sees a rabbit, sets out to catch it, and many times he will. However, where there are thickets and holes he loses most of his prey. On the other hand, the old blood or blue tick hound is ugly and wrinkled, has long floppy ears, and hunts slowly by scent. He will follow a trail all day and all night. He will go over hills into valleys through thickets and across creeks until he catches up to his prey.

Many Christians are like the greyhound. They are fast and beautiful, so promising; yet they only run as long as they can see the object before them. When they lose sight of it they are ready to give up and head back to the pen. Sometimes they may look down on the lowly old hound. He is slow, built low to the ground, and a little ugly. This reminds me of the problem that we can have in the church at times with the young and the old. Many of the young people have been off to college and have become educated, idealistic, and enthusiastic. They have a vision, and they want to catch it at

1

once. This can be good. They fly by the old hounds that have been on the trail a long time. Youth really ought to stop and salute the older teachers, preachers, elders, and deacons. They've gone over hilltops and through valleys and through thickets and across rivers and they are still going. They need to remember, too, that greyhounds spend most of their lives chasing wooden rabbits that they will never catch and should they catch one they would find that it's nothing but a pine knot.

We need each other. We need youth with its enthusiasm, idealism, and speed. We need the older Christians for their strength, wisdom, and experience. They have gone, when they could not see. They followed when there was only hope. Years ago I had an old bird dog named Jack. It got so I had to help him in and out of the trunk of the car. Some of my friends made fun of him, but he would throw his head in the air and trot off and in just a little bit have the birds pointed. The young dogs ran so beautifully. They cut the fields up, but they would honor old Jack by backing him.

Let's remember, "We walk by faith and not by sight." We walk by understanding and compassion, not pride. We walk by love and patience, not criticism. God never said we had to be first, only to be steady. We have the scent of the fragrance of the love of God in Christ Jesus our Lord. Follow it all the way home.

Open Your Gifts

IMAGINE A FATHER WHO WENT OUT TO FIND HIS children very special gifts that he knew they would enjoy and needed. He spent hours searching for just the right thing. Finally when he had found the gifts he carefully and beautifully wrapped them and put their names on them and placed them under the tree. Finally, Christmas morning came and the children came down the stairs, the father passed the presents out with great excitement and enthusiasm, but when the children received their presents they put them aside and didn't even bother to open them. One even threw his present into the fire. The father was disappointed and brokenhearted over the indifference of the children toward the gifts that he had specially purchased for each one of them. What is wrong, he thought? Where is the joy and enthusiasm and curiosity? The children went back upstairs and went to bed.

Can you imagine the disappointment of the Heavenly Father who had just the right gift to fit all of the needs of the world to heal our mental, physical, moral, and social illnesses, to teach us to love one another, to know the peace and the joy that the Father had intended for us? Yes, even to forgive us and free us of the bondage of sin and death.

Some never even bother to open the gift, to look at Jesus, to read His wonderful words, nor to take Him into their lives. But, even worse than this, some took the gift and threw it as it were into the fire for many said, "Let him be crucified. We have no king but Caesar."

But, those of us in the church say we would never do something like this, but how many in the church have been given wonderful gifts and talents that they have never opened, never used? Gifts that could enrich their lives and the lives of others are still unopened, untouched, and unused. How it must break His heart!

Just as we will open our gifts this Christmas with excitement and enthusiasm, let us open, appreciate, enjoy, and use the gifts God has so generously given to us.

Don't Despise All Annoyances

WE TEND TO FUME AND FUSS ABOUT ALL THE LITTLE annoyances of life, but they may have a very important purpose. The rhinoceros, for example, is big, powerful, fast, and fearless. The rhinoceros, however, is infested with many ticks that pierce into his tough hide. I am sure this annoys him and he probably rolls in the dirt trying to remove them, but to little avail. But, what he may not know is that these ticks attract a tick bird about the size of a starling. These birds ride on his back pulling the ticks.

Now the real advantage is this. The rhinoceros has very poor eyesight. The tick bird is his alarm system. Having excellent eyesight they warn the rhinoceros when danger is near.

Isn't it wonderful how God has planned in His creation that we complement each other? That God in so many ways has compensated for our weaknesses. We should learn from this not to fuss and fume all of the time about our difficulties and annoyances but try to realize that good may come from them. You see, a tick is not nearly as dangerous to a rhinoceros as a man with a high-powered rifle.

Weaknesses and annoyances can keep us from pride and vanity. Paul saw his thorn in the flesh as a buffet to his being overly exalted. He had been caught up into paradise and heard unspeakable words. He prayed about it three times that it might be removed. God told him, "My power is made perfect in weakness." Paul accepted it gladly. "I will glory in my weakness ... for when I am weak then am I strong" (2 Corinthians 12: 1–10). This reminds me of Naaman in the Old Testament who was a mighty man of valor, a courageous soldier, but he was a leper. But, that leprosy would bring him in contact with the man of God and this would change his life forever (2 Kings 5:1).

This reminds me of the church. We are a body. We complement each other. One may have the good eyes and another a wonderful voice and another good ears, another strong hands, and another swift feet. Put these all together and add the spirit of Christ, and we have an invincible team. So we have a choice in life in regard to our weaknesses and our annoyances. We can fuss and cuss, or we can try to see good that might come of our troubles.

What Class Passenger?

A MAN OF MODEST MEANS WAS ABOUT TO TAKE A LONG journey old stagecoach. He was informed when he went to buy his ticket that there were three, classes: first class, second class, and third class passengers. When they showed him the seats on the coach the seats all looked alike to him, so he purchased a third class ticket. All went well for a time and he was complimenting himself on how much money he had saved and wondering what difference there was in the first-class and third-class ticket. About that time the stagecoach reached the foot of a very steep hill. Then the driver stopped the horses and shouted, "First-class passengers keep your seats, second-class get out and walk, third-class get out and push." Then he found the meaning of the third-class passenger.

There are a lot of high hills facing the church on its homeward destination. The church is in an uphill battle without any doubt. There are those who consider themselves first-class passengers. When the church is straining to get over the steep hill, they, without any apology, keep their seats and ride over. There are others in the church who will get out and walk and at least take their weight off the gospel coach. Then there are those who will not only get out but will push to help the church get over the steep hill. Unlike the western old stagecoach, there are no classes of passengers. Paul said, "There can be neither Jew nor Greek, bond nor free, male nor female, for we are all one in Christ" (Galatians 3:28). Again, he says, "Who maketh thee to differ from another" (1 Corinthians 4:7). You see, we all ride third-class. We must all be ready to get out and push. Churches that never grow nor reach their destination are churches filled with first-class passengers. The early church must have been filled with people who rode third-class because they would push, pull or lift to keep the church moving toward its destiny — men like Paul and Barnabas and Steven and Peter — women like Dorcas and Lydia. What class passenger are you?

Victims of Our Success

WALMART STARTED OUT WITH ONE SMALL STORE IN Arkansas. Mr. Walton only wanted a few more stores. Then somehow it caught on and grew and grew. Now there are hundreds in this country and others scattered in parts of the world.

We stopped the other night to get baby formula for little Bob. We passed by Walmart. My son said, "I'd rather pay fifty cents more and get it here than to find a parking place and stand in line." Even success has a downside. I see a lot of people doing this now. And in the shadow of the giant Super Centers neighborhood Dollar Stores are springing up and doing well. Is Walmart a victim of its own success?

I think we are seeing this today in our country. This is not what the Pilgrims had in mind when they came here. The country was small, God-fearing, and struggling to survive, but today we are crowded, divided, irritable, fighting with one another, and long lines of traffic, pollution, social disorder, and crime. Have we become victims of our own success?

The same might be true of individuals. Early on we were happy just to have food. Now it must be special food prepared in special ways. There was a time when we were happy just to have shelter, something out of the rain, heat, and cold, but now we are not happy unless the curtains and the carpet match. There was a time when we said if we could just have water inside the house. Now we are not happy unless it flows from gold-colored faucets. Oh, if we could have indoor toilets we would never ask for anything else, but now we can't enjoy them unless they match the hot tub. But in our quest for more and more, who's happy, who's content, and who's thankful? We, too, are victims of our own success. I try to remember that Jesus said, "Give us this day our daily bread" (Matthew 6:11). And Paul said, "Having food and raiment let us therewith be content" (1 Timothy 6:8).

Even the church, it seems, has become a victim of its own success. Many have just about filled up their pews. Thus we could become indifferent about the lost.

What I Learned at the Grocery Store

WHILE JAN WAS DOWN WITH HER FOOT SURGERY, I HAD to go to the grocery store among other things. I learned quickly that I knew nothing about buying groceries. I knew nothing about where things were. I knew nothing about prices. I thought they had made a mistake on the milk. The last milk I bought was $1.49. There was sticker shock on everything.

Then I felt like people were looking at me as if to say, "What are you doing here?" I always believed that women did the grocery buying. My dad never bought groceries. When I got in line there was a woman behind me who looked at my groceries and then looked at me kind of funny like. I felt like I needed to explain this to her. I said, "My wife had foot surgery and I am having to buy the groceries now." She said, "Lord, I have had hip surgery, knee replacement, and I have to go back next week for more surgery. I wish I had someone to buy my groceries." I didn't tell Jan about this. I thought it might hurt her feelings. Then, too, I read that older women go to the grocery store sometimes looking for older men buying groceries, but I didn't believe that.

But what really caught my eye was this: A man in front of me (see there were other men there) bought a carton of cigarettes and a six-pack of beer, and it cost more than the groceries I had bought, including bread and milk and a couple of other items. I breathed a quiet prayer to say to my Father, "Thank you Lord for getting me past these addictions." I did not drink nor smoke because I had such great willpower, but rather because I had made a commitment to the Lord to preach the gospel and I knew there was no place for either. I thought, too, how much I had saved in both money and health by not smoking or drinking over say, 55 years.

Well, thankfully, Jan is up again going to the store and how sweet it is, but now I may be wondering if there are older men looking for older, I mean younger, women at the grocery store.

Called Up

My CHILDREN AND SO MANY OF US IN THIS AREA KEEP up with the progress of Josh Willingham who has been in the farm club of the Florida Marlins. He is a Mars Hill graduate and a star baseball player for UNA. While we were all excited when he was called up to the major leagues, he is not starting every day but he is there. You get called up usually when someone gets hurt or you are played so well in the minor league. His seems to be the latter.

The downside, of course, is you may have to go back down to the minors. I don't see how they deal with the pressure, but what do you do when you have to go back down? Well, you can quit or do your best again. He seems to do his best.

So it is in life. You are called up; you are sent back down. We have our highs and our lows. We have to prepare for both. Paul said it best in Philippians 4:11, "I have learned in whatever state therewith to be content." May we put the rest of what he said like this, "I have learned how to deal with being called up and how to deal with being sent back down. I can handle both with Christ who strengthens me." Paul says again in 2 Corinthians 12:2–12. "He was caught up (like called up) and saw unspeakable things." The first temptation was to boast. He said, "I will not." Of course, you know he had to come back down. He said, "I will glory in my weakness, my disappointments for when I am weak then I am strong." God help us to handle our highs and lows like this.

I also think called up is a wonderful expression of Christian death. Someone said to me, who did not know my brother, Lamar, had died, "Where is your brother now?" "Oh, he has been called up to the majors." Would they not say, "How great!" I hope my children can answer someday when someone asks, "Where are your Dad and your Mother?" "Oh, they have been called up to the majors." I don't think they would say, "Oh, I am so sorry." But rather, "How wonderful!"

My Mother Was Ahead of the Times

I saw a young man pull up the other day in a nice sports car that probably cost well over $20,000. He had on a pair of old faded jeans with holes in the knees. My first thought was that he must have stolen the car, but somebody told me, "No, that's the style." And I thought I wore old jeans with patches and holes because we were poor. My mother was just a little ahead of the times. She tried to tell us how nice we looked, but I never believed her. If I were in school today, I would be the best-dressed boy. The old look in my pants came from somebody else using them first.

Can you believe it? For most of my life, we ate vegetables and cornbread. Now, how in the world did my mother know about cholesterol and red meats? We were vegetarians before it was popular. And I had the strange notion it was because we were poor, but my mother was way ahead of the times.

I thought she spanked us because she didn't have time to sit down and reason with us. One of the best sellers today in parenting is *Love Must Be Tough*. My mother knew that. She didn't have time to read all the books on reasoning with children.

We hear a lot today about exercise and the value that it brings to the cardiovascular system. When we were growing up you didn't see people walking around the block for exercise. They were too tired from working hard all day. They didn't have to take pills to go to sleep at night either. Mother kept us exercising most of the time, and I thought all the time it was because there was so much to be done. Mother knew an idle mind was the devil's workshop.

We are told now that young people need role models to look to, someone they can believe in, goals, inspiration, and hope for their lives. My mother knew that. She showed us Jesus and taught us of Him. We worshiped together, read the Bible together, and prayed together.

I am kidding, of course, when I say that Mother knew about cholesterol and such things, but I am not kidding when I say that Christian mothers are ahead of their times because they are in tune with God and they have a wonderful book of instructions from Him. Could Paul have had this in mind when he said, "Children obey your parents in the Lord for this is right. Honor thy father and mother which is the first commandment with promise, that it may be well with thee and that thou mayest live long on the earth" (Ephesians 6:1).

A Twenty Minute Door

Richard Hall was telling me the other day about bidding on a school building where the specifications called for fire retardant doors. He asked them if they wanted twenty minute doors or three hour doors. A twenty minute door is designed to retard the fire for that length of time and a three hour door for three hours. Of course, price always figures into that. The longer it can hold the fire off the more expensive it is.

In figuring what kind of door you want you have to ask yourself what is at stake. There may be twenty or thirty young people behind each of these doors. A three hour door might give the fire department time to get there and save the children. Whether it is a twenty minute door or a three hour door may make the difference in life or death.

Fire is such a devastating force. Besides the burning flame you have heat and smoke, plus chemicals from the material it is burning. To have something between you and the raging fire could be worth everything. Peter gives a graphic description of the second coming of Jesus Christ. He says, "The elements shall be dissolved with fervent heat and the earth and the works that are therein shall be burned up ... by reason of which the heavens being on fire shall be dissolved and the elements melt with fervent heat" (2 Peter 3).

Isn't it comforting to know at that time you have a door between you and this devastating destruction — not a twenty minute or three hour door. Jesus so beautifully says, "I am the door, by me if any man enter in he shall be saved and shall go in and out and find pasture" (John 10:9). Paul talks of this protective door at the end of the world in 1 Thessalonians 4: 17, "Then we that are alive that are left shall together with them be caught up in the clouds to meet the Lord in the air and so shall we ever be with the Lord." Have you put your hope, your dreams, your security behind a twenty minute door? The rich man of Luke 16 cried and said, "Father Abraham, have mercy on me and send Lazarus that he may dip the tip of his finger in water and cool my tongue for I am in anguish in this flame." You see, he only had a twenty minute door. How about you?

I'm Fasting Today

DURING THE WAR OF THE CRUSADERS A CAPTAIN WHO knew they were outnumbered and they would surely die that day, told his men, "All who die today will sup with Christ in paradise." The officer himself started walking away and one of the soldiers asked, "Don't you want to have supper with Christ in paradise?" He said, "Oh, yes, but I'm fasting today." If he had been one of the television evangelists he might have said, "Let me keep your rings and your gold and silver for you." It is a sad thing when captains, leaders, teachers, and preachers send men onto the battlefield rather than lead them, asking people to give their lives, their money, and their savings while they themselves are interested in a paradise on earth. Children many times have been asked by their parents to live right and to do right while the parents excuse themselves from doing what they were asking the children to do. The captain and many others use religion to their advantage. If it is convenient to fast, then fast. The truth of the matter is that he thought this cause was worth somebody dying for, but not himself.

Jesus never sent men where He Himself was not willing to go. When He went into the final battle He did not ask anyone to go with Him. It ended in His death. He said, "Follow me." The apostle Paul was in front of his troops in all the major battles. "I have fought the good fight, I have finished the course, I have kept the faith" (2 Timothy 4:7). Our religious ceremonies may cost us heaven. Are we walking away while others must fight and die alone? Are we talking and singing about heaven but had much rather stay on earth? Are we like the captain covering the real truth — I am not ready or prepared to die? We don't need to be fasting. We should be fighting.

Thirty Minutes to Pack

THE FIREMAN RUSHED TO THE DOOR AND YELLED, "THE wind has changed. The fire is heading in this direction, and you have about thirty minutes to get out." You may have seen this a few weeks ago on the news. The forest fires were devasting the countryside with no end in sight. This house looked to be worth a quarter of a million dollars. It was well planned. There was a beautiful view. It surely was tastefully furnished. How quickly the beautiful things of life can turn on us. The beautiful trees and landscape will bring the fire to the door. If you had thirty minutes to run in and grab a few things, what would you get? Maybe the real question is, "What would you leave?" Suddenly, life forces some hard decisions. All at once we have to get our priorities straight. Many have told of getting worthless things and leaving the valuable things behind. The real things of life you cannot put in a suitcase. They are in one's heart, mind, locked in one's memory. The valuable things of life cannot be burned in a fire or washed away in a flood or blown away in the wind. You can't burn love and deeds and thoughts. They were blessed to get out with their lives.

We, too, are under a fire alert. Peter says, " ... the elements shall be dissolved with fervent heat and the earth and the works that are therein shall be burned up." We, too, have a warning. It raises a question, "Seeing that these things are thus all to be dissolved, what manner of persons ought ye to be in all holy living and godliness." Amidst all of the ruin and devastation, there is yet hope. Peter continues, "But according to His promise we look for a new heaven and a new earth wherein dwelleth righteousness." Jesus said, "In my Father's house are many rooms." We have been warned. Thank God that we had a warning, that we had a way of escape, that we have hope and the promise of rebuilding again with Christ. Who knows how long we have to get out of this world? We need to be ready at all times.

A Unique Mission

Someone has said that Alexander went forth to conquer the world. Caesar went forth to battle, due to his enemies. Plato and Socrates went forth in search of knowledge. Columbus went forth to discover the new world. Stanley went forth to explore Africa. Warriors have gone forth to rout armies and their march has been tracked with blood, misery, and death. Expeditions have gone forth to explore distant regions, to see the wonders of nature, and view the monuments of arts. Philanthropists have gone forth on errands of mercy.

And I might add that men of our day have gone forth to explore the moon and the far reaches of outer space. Men have found oil on the floor of the sea and now they have gone forth into the microscopic world of genes and DNA.

But the most unique quest is stated in one short line, "Christ came to seek and save the lost" (Luke 19:10). He did not come to conquer the world but to save it. He did not come in search of knowledge but to impart it. He did not come in search of a world but to impart a new life. He did not come to rout armies but to disband them. He did not come in search of treasure but rather to tell us where to invest ours. He did not come to the world to condemn it but to save it. He did not come to this earth to destroy but to build upon it His church.

What should be the mission of the church of Christ today? Should it not be to seek and to save the lost? Our mission is not to reconcile Christ to our world but reconcile our world to Christ. Neither is our mission the mission of merely accumulating religious knowledge but rather the proclaiming of the Gospel of Christ. The church like Jesus should feed the hungry and heal the sick and care for the widows and orphans, but we must never forget what this was to Jesus and should be to us a means to this end, saving the lost. Too often the church has been bowed down with a social agenda and people died full, clothed, and well, but lost. If the church does not concern itself with the spiritual needs of the work, then who will? His mission is our mission "to seek and save the lost."

Older Brother But Not the Elder Brother

WE KNOW THE STORY OF THE ELDER BROTHER TOLD BY Jesus in Luke 15. He was the brother who stayed home, the one who would never go to the far country, the one, in fact, who was in the field when the prodigal brother came home. But there was something bad in the elder brother's heart. There was envy, suspicion, bitterness, and littleness, teaching us that you do not have to go to the far country to be lost. Many are lost at home.

Lamar was nine years older than I, and the oldest of nine, but he had none of the qualities of the elder brother. He was always eager to believe the best, always the last to expose. He would have welcomed the prodigal with open arms. He would have celebrated with the father at the boy's return. He would have been praying for his younger brother and did.

Lamar would have been 80 on July 20th (July 20, 2001). There was a great family celebration planned. He was looking forward to it. We never know about that next birthday.

He meant more to me than even I knew. He was there

25

for me when I was a teen. Mother sent me to Illinois to spend the summer with him. It was there I decided I wanted to preach like my older brother. He was there for me when we got married. We were married there in their house. Chloe went all out for the wedding. She showed Jan many things. What I dread is this: Lamar won't be there for my children when Jan and I pass on. They will miss him.

I would never have come to Tuscumbia, had it not been for Lamar. Brother Charlie Morris asked Lamar, "Do you know where we could get a preacher?" He said, "My brother, Bob, might come." Brother Morris said, "Can he preach?" I told them at the funeral Lamar said, "He's real nice." But I was joking. Brother Morris told me what Lamar said. He said, "He is a better preacher than I." He was joking, too.

My children and grandchildren loved "Uncle 'Mar." One of them said they were going to school at Uncle Mar's Hill. My five year old granddaughter heard her mother and daddy talking about whether to take them or not and she said emphatically, "I am going to Uncle 'Mars graduation." He was loved by so many, young and old alike.

Where Could I Go?

THERE IS AN OLD HYMN IN OUR SONGBOOKS THAT SAYS, "Yet when I face the chilling hand of death, where could I go but to the Lord?" I think we saw this in the days after the attack on our nation. It was so overwhelming, so unbelievable that most people cried out, "Oh, God, help us."

There are times when some people rush to the bar, but a drink was not going to fix this. One bar closed leaving a note "Gone to pray."

So many times we turn to the government for help, but it was the government that was under attack. The President himself was in flight, trying to find a secure place where he could assess what was happening and find the best solution.

I doubt that anyone rushed to the psychiatrist for help. We did not need someone to tell us what the problem was, we knew. We needed someone who had the power and the strength to get us through it.

I think we all realized at this time that no amount of money could fix this. It can't bring lives back. No amount of money could undo the damage nor heal our broken hearts.

I didn't hear of anyone running to the science laboratories for answers or comfort. They can transplant a heart, but only Jesus can transform it and make the broken heart smile again and love again.

The President called for a day of prayer and remembrance. How sad, our children who were in public schools that day could not participate because it is against the law.

In times like these we seem to be like children who, when they are hurt say, "I want my father. I want my mother." No one else will do. God tells His people, "As a mother comforts her child, so I will comfort you" (Isaiah 66:13).

800 Nitpickers

One of the leading American car manufacturers advertised in a national magazine that they had 800 nitpickers. The scene was eight to ten men carefully examining one car. They say, "If we do not nitpick, you will not pick our car."

Maybe we need some nitpickers. Nitpicking can be good if one is looking at one's own product. Paul said, in regard to eating the Lord's Supper, "But let a man examine himself ... let him eat" (1 Corinthians 11:28).

Paul says in 1 Corinthians 9: 27: "But I buffet my body and bring it into bondage, lest by any means, after that I preached to others, I myself should be rejected."

Too much of our nitpicking has been directed toward others. There is little benefit derived from this. It leads to strife, not quality. Nitpicking could be good for a marriage if each would examine himself or herself.

If you are one of the 800 nitpickers, start in your own mirror. Remember, personal quality is job one.

The Because People

CHARLES OSGOOD WAS JOKING ABOUT THE *BECAUSE people* on the radio the other day. It seems there was a mistake in the economic report. The report stated that productivity was down. So the *because people* cited all the reasons productivity was down. Then they learned this was a mistake and productivity was really up. Then they listed all the reasons it was up. The same thing happened with the unemployment figures. The report said that unemployment was rising. The *because people* said. "here are the reasons it is rising." When they found out it was down, they listed the reasons why unemployment was down. So much for the *because people*.

This led me to do a little thinking on my own. Tbe *because people* have been noticing the drought in the west. So the *because people* predict that we are in another "Dust Bowl Era." They say it is because the great Rain Forest in the Amazon Basin and other places around the world are being destroyed. And because in this country we are clearing so

30

much land for farming and laying more asphalt for parking lots and buildings. And yet we are having flood conditions all over the country this year, even in California. One man wondered how much deeper the water would have been in his den if they hadn't cut the Rain Forest. The *because people* were having a convention on global warming a couple of winters ago. During that time records were broken all over the country. In some places, the wind chill was 80 degrees below zero. You remember that December when all the pipes froze? I am not saying there is not a cause-and-effect relationship in this, it may well be. I don't think we know yet what causes floods and droughts. We just mop the water or wipe the dust.

Look at the economic experts. They miss more than they hit as to what is going to take place. They said everyone would start spending after Dessert Storm, but it didn't happen.

Now I have said all that to say this. When the experts tell us that there is life on earth because of a great bang or explosion and that we evolved through natural selection and survival of the fittest. I wouldn't run right out and get a machine gun so you could be one of the fittest and survive. It was the educated experts who told us that man would get better. kinder, and gentle, through evolution. Look at Iraq, Ethiopia, and South Africa just to name a few. It's from the experts that we are told the Bible could not be the word of God because there is no God. And why are you sure there is no God? "Because we do not like, nor believe the Bible." And why do you not like the Bible? "Because it says man is accountable." There will be a day of judgment and punishment for the wicked. We should take the *because people* with a grain of salt. Paul said, "Where is the wise ... where is the disputer of the world? Hath not God made foolishness the wisdom of the world" (1 Corinthians 1:20).

Fat Free

HELPING JAN TAKE THE GROCERIES OUT OF THE CAR I said. "You must have saved a bundle today. Half of what you bought says 'free' on it. You have free mayonnaise, free margarine, free salad dressing, free ice cream, free potato chips, free bread." She said, "Oh no, that just means fat or cholesterol free." It actually costs more and tastes less. I did hear about a man who took a sack and put some of these free items in it and walked out. They caught him at the door. He told them it was free. It said so in plain English. I don't know how it will come out.

There is a move on today, however, to get the fat out. We are moving toward leaner things not only in food but in the workplace. Large corporations are restructuring to get the fat out. It's going to be painful because there are many layoffs and pink slips. The outside world is pushing us to be more productive and efficient. Even the government is trying to take the fat out, but they seem to put three layers in for every layer they take out. This is happening in the state, county, and city governments as well. Hopefully, if we can ever get over the pain of it, we will all be better off. Fast food chains are trying to get the fat out. There are new lean hamburgers. The skin is being taken off of the chicken. Diet centers are booming.

It seems to be that it's high time for churches and preachers to get the fat out and offer a fat-free gospel. The gospel of Jesus Christ came to us lean. You notice in the teaching of Jesus the economy of words. John said,

> Many other signs therefore did Jesus in the presence of the disciples which are not written in this book, but these are written that ye may believe that Jesus is the Christ the Son of God and that believing ye might have life in His name (John 20:30–31).

Again he says, "And there are also many other things which Jesus did the which if they should be written every one I suppose that even the world itself would not contain the books thr1t should be written" (John 21:25). As great as were the words and deeds of Jesus Christ, they were edited by the Holy Spirit to give us a lean, all-sufficient lifesaving gospel. The early church kept the gospel lean. Men have added creeds, dogmas, traditions, opinions, and innovations. You can't have lean and healthy Christians until you have a fat-free gospel. The church could be in the shape it's in because of what it is being fed. Paul charged young Timothy in the sign of God and of Jesus Christ to preach the word. (2 Timothy 4:1) That may be another way of saying, "Keep the fat out."

Goals Reached At Forty?

A FEW WEEKS AGO LEE ATWATER DIED OF A BRAIN tumor at the age of forty. Anyone who followed the news at all will remember Lee Atwater. He was full of life and energy. He was ambitious and enthusiastic. About a year before his death a brain tumor was discovered. He spent the last year fighting for his life. The thing that struck me about Lee Atwater was the fact that he said, "There are two goals in my life, and I have reached them both." One was to run a presidential campaign and to win and he did. The other was to be the chairman of his party, and he was.

This reminded me of a few things about goals. First, select good and worthy goals for your life because you will probably reach them. We need some direction in which to aim our lives.

So many people are goalless in life. All of the great men had a sense of mission and purpose in life. We need preparation to reach our goals. This can involve education, experience, and training. We need, as he did, to define our goals and make them definite. There can be no doubt that he had reached them.

Many, like Lee Atwater, need to re-evaluate their goals. When the brain tumor was discovered, he was told he had about a year to live. Lee Atwater spent most of the last year of his life apologizing to people for the way he reached his goals. His new goal life had was to make peace with himself, his enemies, and God. He had to re-evaluate his goals in the light of death and the judgment. We must set our goals with the consideration of others in mind, our families, our fellow-man, and above all our Lord.

If you should be told today that you had a year to live, what goals have you reached? What changes would you make? What would then be your priorities? The apostle Paul said, "For me to live is Christ and to die is gain" (Philippians 1:21). Paul was set whether he lived or died.

That's My Seat

SEATING IS A PROBLEM ANYWHERE PEOPLE ARE gathered. The only reason Jesus didn't have any problem with it when he fed the five thousand was because there were no seats. Seats are assigned by number to people who buy tickets to sporting events or airline flights. Schools solve their seating problems the same way. The problem, however, is a little different in the church assemblies.

THE CHRISTIAN CHRONICLE carried this story about a California denominational church and how they coped with the problem. "It seems they had to assign seats when church members became possessive with their pews. Missionary Blake Withers told about meeting a church prospect in a grocery store. The contact and his wife visited the service in Withers' congregation the next Sunday, but the visitors left when a member informed them that they were sitting in the member's seat. Withers was disturbed when he discovered what had happened. He got the visitors' phone number and called to advise them that four seats were available on the second row. He then asked, 'Could you use the other two?' The prospects came the next Sunday morning and brought two friends. All four are now active members of the church."

Not many incidents like this have a happy ending. More times than not people who are treated like this never, never come back. The strange irony is that everywhere but the church people want the front seats. Our problems are always from the middle to the back of the church building. A full house would be a wonderful problem for the church to cope with. There are so many empty church buildings in our land.

There are times when people need special seats. There are people with health problems who need to be near the back where they can get up and go out without disturbing others. Mothers with babies may need some of these back seats. There are people who need seats near the front where they see better and hear better.

Jan and I might start sitting in a different seat to let it be known that these are not our exclusive seats. I think there is some merit to members finding a place that's comfortable for them and sitting there from week to week, but it's tragic to ask a visitor to get up because "You are in my seat." Mary knew it wasn't where she sat but before whom she sat. Mary sat at Jesus's feet (Luke 10:39). Remember it was the Pharisees who had their special seats (Luke 20:46). The only seat that is really yours is the one right behind your backbone!

My Mother's Perfect

Did you read about the small boy who walked into a lingerie section of a large department store and shyly presented his problem to a woman clerk in that department. "I want to buy a slip as a present for my mom," he said. "But l don't know what size she wears." He had overheard his mother talking about needing a new slip. The clerk asked, "Is she tall or short, heavy or skinny?" He said, "She's just perfect." He smiled from ear to ear so the clerk reached up and got a size 34 and wrapped it for him. Two days later his mother came into the store by herself and changed the slip to a size 52. You see this little boy did not notice or care about the size. His mother was perfect in kindness and love and caring. His mother had a 34 heart. Maybe children look and evaluate more as God does — by the heart.

Samuel was told, "The Lord seeth not as man seeth, man looketh on the outward appearance. but the Lord looks on the heart" (1 Samuel 16:7). Our world has become victimized by sizes and numbers and dimensions. Very seldom do we pay attention to what is within a man or a woman. We have some dear friends in South Carolina. The wife gained a little too much weight, and the husband would tease her a little bit it. She would turn to him and say. "I'm gonna die one of these days, and you can marry about you a little ole mean skinny woman." Of course, we should all be conscious of our health and the way we eat and exercise, but it seems to be true that we come in different shapes and sizes.

Mothers, how do your children really feel about you? You can't get much higher marks than these. Remember, it isn't what the world thinks about you. It's what your children think. Many mothers have high marks out in the marketplace but low marks among those who know them best. Who is this perfect mother, anyway? She loves. She cares. She gives. She forgives. She disciplines. She holds. She wipes tears and other places. She binds up wounds. She turns a house into a home. She can take a few groceries and turn them into a delicious meal. She reads to them from God's word and takes them to God's house. Then one day she gently and perhaps reluctantly releases them to fly on their own.

"Mother, did you ever know that you are my hero? You are everything I'd like to be. I can fly higher than an eagle, but you are the wind beneath my wings."

Love Gas, Why Not?

It occurred to me in the height of the Persian Gulf War when men were terrorized by the thought of chemical warfare, gases that could blister, disable, and cause agonizing death why could we not come up with a love gas? We have a gas that will make you cry, tear gas, gas to make you laugh, a gas that will make you sleep, a gas that will keep you warm, a gas that will cut through plate steel, a gas that will make a plane fly and a car run and even a gas for execution. Why have we not, with all our genius, been able to make a gas that would make us kind, gentle, and loving; a gas that would turn us to each other, help us to see the good in each other; a gas that would remove hate, greed, lust, selfishness, pride, and prejudice. The reason is — man is bent on destruction. It is easier it seems to make weapons of destruction rather than instruments of peace.

How desperately we need such a gas today. One of the canisters could be dropped on the border of Israel, Jordan, and Syria. Another in Iraq and Northern Ireland, South Africa, Ethiopia, Libya, the Philippines, and the Republics

41

of the Soviet Union. We need this gas on the streets of our own cities where crimes of violence occur every few seconds.

Yes, and we need this gas in the home. Homes are breaking up. Violence and abuse are rampant in the home. We need a gas that will make husbands and wives cling to each other, and children who are sweet, gentle, and kind. Sadly, we need this gas in the church where we have division, confusion, pride, and self-centeredness.

We have such a gas or influence. Isaiah predicted it in Isaiah 2:4, "They shall beat their swords into plowshares and their spears into pruning hooks. Nation shall not lift up sword against nation. Neither shall they learn war anymore." It was taught and demonstrated by Jesus Christ. He said, "Love one another as I have loved you." He taught the fatherhood of God and the brotherhood of man. He changed rough fishermen into apostles of love and peace. Jesus changed a chained, naked demoniac into one sitting at his feet clothed and in his right mind. It was demonstrated in the early church where Jews and Gentiles sat down together in one family. This power melted the most vicious enemy of the church, Saul of Tarsus, who became the greatest ambassador and missionary of truth, love, and peace. I see this power at work today in Christian hearts and homes.

Why, then, is there so much hate? Satan has made a mask to resist this love. Paul said, "Even if our gospel is veiled, it is veiled in them that perish in whom the God of this world hath blinded the minds of the unbelieving that the light of the gospel of the glory of Christ who is the image of God should not dawn upon them." Lord, may the spirit of Christ penetrate our hearts, our homes, and our world before it is forever too late.

The Crop Laid By

I'VE HEARD THIS OLD PHRASE MOST OF MY LIFE FROM farmers and gardeners. It means the crop is planted and the farmer has done about all he can do. He has worked to prepare the ground. He has loosened the soil with his plow. He has carefully planted the seed. He has applied the appropriate amount of fertilizer. He has hoed the weeds from the tender plants. The rest is up to God, they say. This seems to be biblically sound. Paul said in 1 Corinthians 3:6, "I have planted, Apollos watered, but God giveth the increase." Paul further says that "We are fellow laborers together with God." We are not in this alone. What a big and generous partner is God. Man cannot make seed, he can only plant it. Neither can we make Christians, we can only plant the word. Here is power and potential for which man must wait, for which man has no control. Some think, however, this is a layaway plan. You lay the seed away in a drawer and sit in your recliner and hope that someone will share the harvest with you. I've never gotten my garden to lay by. The grass and the weeds never stop. There is some work to do it seems until the harvest comes.

There is a principle in life that we need to recognize. This is what Paul had in mind when he said, "I have planted, Apollos watered, but God gives the increase." There is just so much we can do in life to bring the harvest to pass. Paul was talking about his own spiritual disappointments and frustrations. Preachers and teachers face the same today. Paul came to realize that which we must all realize. That is, we must plant the seed and hope and pray that the soil is good and honest. It won't help to walk the floor, to sleep with it, to watch it constantly, to remove the dirt when the first little shoot breaks through. The seed will do this. Jesus said, "The Kingdom is like a man casting seed upon the earth and he should sleep and rest night and day and the seed should spring up and grow. He knoweth not how" (Matthew 4:26–27). Simply saying we don't have to understand it nor to explain it to enjoy the wonderful fruit thereof. Do your part and go to bed and let God do his. Paul learned to rely on God and said in Galatians 6:9, "And let us not be weary in well doing for in due season we shall reap if we faint not."

Wrapped Up In What?

HE WAS GOING TO TAKE THE KIDS TO SCHOOL ON HIS WAY to work. They were running a little late. When they started toward the car they saw that the back tire was flat. He kicked the tire firmly and said, "But it's a steel belted radial. You remember they were billed as the tires that were puncture-proof. It seems that I've had as many flats on the steel belted as any tire. They are good against the large objects but a small screw or a small nail will go right into them." This seems to be true in life. Many protect themselves from the elephant and the tiger, but it's the ant and tick that seem to do the damage.

Never has there been a time when mankind has sought security against all the hazards of life as we see today. He literally wants to be wrapped in steel or something to protect him. Some have steel bars on the doors and windows. The security business is one of the fastest-growing businesses in America. Some wrap themselves in electronics, sophisticated devices that will sound an alarm when anyone tampers with a house or car.

Others simply wrap themselves in insurance. They cover everything. One insurance advertises the security blanket. Others wrap themselves in gold and silver and precious metals. They feel more secure with gold than steel. Still others wrap themselves in furs and diamonds and expensive jewelry. Still others wrap themselves in vitamins. They feel that the best security is good health and fitness. They walk. They run. They eat right. Billions around the world wrap themselves in religion. They put their hope and trust in men; men they believe are divine. Many are wrapping themselves in education and knowledge. Too many today are wrapping themselves in armament. History, experience, observation, and revelation teach us that all these within themselves will not protect nor save. Amos says it's like a man fleeing from a lion only to meet a bear and finally he reaches his house of safety and rests his hand on the wall only to have a small serpent bite him. (Amos 5: 19)

Since our first parents sinned men have been looking for a covering and leaves were insufficient. Men have cried out for covering. David said, "Cover me under the shadow of thy wings" (Psalm 17:8). The only true security blanket is Jesus Christ the Son of God. This is why the Bible urges us to put Christ on (Romans 14:13). And how do we put him on? "For as many of you as were baptized into Jesus Christ did put on Christ" (Galatians 3:27). In what are you wrapped? Many times that which we trust fails us when we need it most.

Out of the Mouths of Babes

My grandson has an insatiable appetite for sweets. I took him aside the other day and told him how bad sweets were for him. I said, "If you keep eating all of these sweets, you won't grow up to be big and strong. You won't be able to go fishing with me. I told him that sweets would cause his teeth to decay and fall out. I concluded by telling him that "gum, cookies, and candy are just old junk." He looked up at me, with his big, blue eyes and, as sober and sincerely as anyone could say, "Paw Paw, I yike junk!" He can't pronounce his ls. I thought to myself, how honest children are. You know, he might have said, if he had been a little bit older, "Think of all the quick energy I can get from sweets." He just told the honest truth, "I yike junk!"

We, as adults, won't admit that we like junk. We like to kid ourselves and to fool others. Ask a man, "Why do you drink alcoholic beverages?" Many times we are told, "Just to be more sociable." Why do you go to these bad movies? Some will say, "Just to get out of the house." Why do you listen to that sorry music? "Oh, there's nothing else on." Why do you

47

read that ugly literature? "Oh, it's educational." Why are you watching those old soap operas on television? "Oh, just to pass the time of day." Why don't we tell it like it is? "Lord, we yike junk!"

Help me to love the good, turn from evil; help me to love your word and to love and appreciate good things. The sooner we stop excusing ourselves and admit the truth, the greater our hope of heaven will be. Paul said, "Abhor that which is evil, cleave to that which is good" (Romans 12:9). "Bread of deceit is sweet to a man; but afterward his mouth shall be filled with gravel" (Proverbs 20:17). "Let no man deceive himself ..." (1 Corinthians 3:18).

The Oreo Kids

We had a wonderful meeting in Decatur with the church at Grant Street. It was good to renew our fellowship with Jim and Marge Wafen and many others. We had dinner together on Sunday. It was their homecoming. They brought their finest foods. The ladies had fixed their special recipes: casseroles of all kinds, chicken, roast, ham and vegetables, and oh, that dessert table — pies and puddings and cherry and chocolate delight, but someone had brought a huge package of Oreos. Would you believe that those young people passed right over those delights and devoured those little black and white cookies? What is wrong with these kids? We ate together another night and a couple of mothers brought cold hot dogs and pizzas. They were claimed before the prayer was offered.

Even more disturbing than this is the junk food for the mind. The movies are shallow, superficial, and dirty with absolutely no moral or spiritual value. I see them advertised or a brief movie review and I can't believe people would pay good money to sec them. The television fare is no better. It's all designed for the sensual.

I guess there's nothing new under the sun, however. When God brought Israel from the mud pits of Egypt they made a gold calf and worshipped it while Moses was in the mountain getting the law from God. Later they rejected God as their king and wanted a man to rule over them. When God sent His son into the world to rescue and save the Jewish people they chose Barabbas and when Pilate said, "What shall I do with Jesus who is called the Christ?" They said, "Let Him be crucified!" When the early church offered love, hope, peace, and pardon they were stoned, beaten, and imprisoned. Man has a history of choosing junk.

And what of our older generation who pick latter day and man made churches over the church that Jesus purchased with His blood? Who pick creeds and disciplines over the inspired word of God. People who are more interested in coffee and donuts than the Lord's Supper. And what about those members of the church who choose magazines and novels over the reading of the Bible? They choose pleasure over Sunday night worship. God said through Moses,

> This day I call heaven and earth as witness against you that I have set before you life and death, blessings and curses. Now choose life so that you and your children may live that you may love the Lord your God, listen to His voice and hold fast to Him (Deuteronomy 30:19–20).

The table of life is set. The choice is up to you.

The Tragedy of Misunderstanding

A DEPARTMENT STORE CLERK WAS DEMONSTRATING THE efficiency of a window-cleaning device by smearing margarine on the glass and cleaning it off again. A woman who was very impressed came by and bought the device. And, as it was being wrapped, she asked, "And how much margarine do I use to get the same results when I get home?" She thought the margarine was a part of the cleaning device. We laugh, but we do the same thing.

Paul had to deal with this same type of problem. In the book of Romans, he was demonstrating how Christ had cleansed us from our transgression and sin. He said, "But where sin did abound grace did abound more exceedingly" (Romans 5:20). It seemed they completely misunderstood this, whether in ignorance or intentionally. They must have thought the more we sin the more God's grace will abound. Or, like the woman, the more margarine I apply to the windows the cleaner they will be. Thus Paul wrote in chapter 6:1, "What shall we say then, shall we continue in sin that grace may abound? God forbid." Sin is not the solution but the problem. Sin is not the cleansing agent but the stain. Paul was shocked at their misunderstanding and said, "Or are ye ignorant that all we who were baptized into Jesus Christ were baptized into his death." The cleansing power is in the blood shed in His death. Then Paul tells them how it was applied, "Ye were buried therefore with him through baptism into death that like as Christ was raised from the dead through the glory of the Father so we also might walk in the newness of life" (Romans 6:4).

Jesus came to show us His cleansing power. Nicodemus who was a ruler of the Jews and a child of Abraham must have thought he was clean and saved. Jesus must have stunned him when he said, "Verily, verily, I say unto you, except one be born anew he cannot see the Kingdom of heaven." Note Nicodemus' misunderstanding, "How can a man be born when he is old? Can he enter a second time into his mother's womb and be born?" Jesus attempted to make it even plainer. "Verily I say unto thee, except one be born of water and the spirit he cannot enter the Kingdom of God." Jesus was shocked at his misunderstanding and said, "Art thou the teacher of Israel and understandest not these things?" Jesus concluded in verse 12 of chapter 3, "If I told you earthly things and ye believed not, how shall ye believe if I tell you heavenly things?" Not only did they miss the new birth. They misunderstood His birth, His mission, His message, His kingdom, His death, His resurrection, and His church. Thus the tragedy of misunderstanding.

With This Ring

June seems to be the most popular month of the year for weddings. You wonder how many times this line has been repeated, "With this ring I do thee wed." It seems to me that we have placed far too much emphasis on the ring. The ring is only a symbol, perhaps the signature of your vows and promises. It seems that many young people have a two or three thousand dollar ring and a two-bit marriage. Their grandparents and parents, perhaps, had a two-bit ring but a million dollar marriage. "With this ring, I promise to love, honor and cherish, for better or worse 'til death do us part." With this ring "forsaking all others I will keep myself for you always." In spite of all these beautiful words and vows half of these marriages will end in divorce, we are told.

About forty-one years ago I worked all summer in a sawmill to buy my wife-to-be a ring. I paid $150.00 for it. I remember it well. It was all I had. We both wished later we had that $150.00 back for that first hard year. Well, maybe I was the only one who wished that. She bought me a gold band for $15.00. I lost my ring a few years after we were married. It is on the bottom of Kentucky Lake, I guess. It slipped off my finger while pulling up an anchor rope. Well, at least I'm consistent. I lost my beautiful David Lipscomb ring also.

The point I make is this. Losing that ring made absolutely no difference in our marriage. I wear my wife in my heart, in my body. We are together as much as we can possibly be. I love to have her at my side. We don't need rings to remind us we are married. Five children and eight grandchildren serve that purpose nicely, thank you. We don't need rings to remind God we are married either. The best repellant to keep predators away from your marriage is not a ring but a healthy, wholesome, loving marriage. If you're not committed to each other and God, the ring will not save your marriage. The piranhas do not respect rings anymore. If you do not know who you are and for what you stand, that ring is worthless and meaningless.

However, our youngest son is about to be married. He told his mother he didn't want to wear an old wedding ring. "Oh," we both said, "You should do that." Then he said, "Dad, you don't wear one." And I said, "But I lost mine. I would like to have a ring." Guess what! Jan went out and bought me one — me and my big mouth. I would like one, but I can't seem to keep up with them.

What did Jesus say about rings? Nothing, but he did say,

> For this cause shall a man leave his father and mother and shall cleave to his wife and the two shall become one flesh ... what therefore God hath joined together let not man put asunder (Matthew 19:5–6).

What did Paul say about the rings? Nothing, but he did say, "Wives, be in subjection to your own husbands as with the Lord. Husbands, love your wives even as Christ also loved the church and gave himself up for it" (Ephesians 5:22–25).

Living Through the Bad Calls
of Life

THE UMPIRE OR THE REFEREE IS A JUDGE. THEY MAKE judgment calls every game. They hardly ever make a call with which both sides agree. Sometimes after a game they need a police escort. Did you ever see an umpire or a referee get a new car or a plaque for his efforts?

Do they make mistakes? Absolutely. The slow-motion instant replay clearly reveals the mistake, but they do not have the option of looking at a slow-motion replay. They have to call it on the spot. There are games lost and won by a bad call, and yet the call stands.

It's hard to deal with the bad calls of life. (Mark) McGuire knocks a home run and they call it a ground rule double. (Michael) Jordan makes two points that would have won the game, but he is called for charging. A beautiful touchdown is called back for holding. One can fuss and cuss and break a bat, throw a chair, or get in the umpire's face, but it won't change the call. I do admire the player who walks back to the dugout, calmly puts his bat and his batting helmet up, and sits down saying, "I've gotten some good calls as well." One should not whine the rest of the game or the rest of his life about a bad call.

Joseph, the son of Jacob, lived through and rose above a bad call. He did not do what Potipher accused him of doing. He served his time. He kept the faith. He did not whine nor complain and for this God opened the prison door for him, and he became exalted in Egypt and was able to feed his own people. Jesus received the worst call ever made. He was called an imposter and a blasphemer, but He rose above it and said, "Father, forgive them for they know not what they do."

Let each of us remember to live through and rise above the bad calls of life.

Thanks for All Things?

In Ephesians 5:20 Paul says, "Giving thanks always for all things in the name of our Lord Jesus Christ, to God even the Father." The Psalmist says, "I will bless the Lord at all times" (34:1). Paul seems to be urging us to take all of life in a spirit of thanksgiving. Thus, giving thanks always for all things. One commentator says we are to give thanks not only for the great but the least favors of God; not only for the new and present benefits but for all we have formerly received; not only for the pleasant blessings but also those which are adverse. Matthew Henry, the great expositor of the Scripture, took this verse to heart when he was robbed by thieves. He said this in his diary,

> Let me be thankful first, because I was never robbed before. Second, because although they took my purse, they did not take my life. Third, because although they took my all, it was not much; and, fourth, because it was I who was robbed, and not I who robbed.

George Matheson, a famous blind preacher of Scotland, prayed on one occasion,

> My God I have never thanked thee for my thorn. I have thanked thee a thousand times for my roses, but never once for my thorns. I have been looking forward to a world where I shall get compensation for my cross as itself present glory. Teach me the glory of, my cross. Teach me the value of pain. Show me that my tears have made my rainbow.

The apostle Paul practiced what he wrote in Ephesians 5:20. He said,

> And by reason of exceeding greatness of the revelations that I should not be exalted over much, there was given to me a thorn in the flesh; a messenger of Satan to buffet me that I should not be exalted over much. Concerning this thing I besought the Lord thrice that it might depart from me and he said unto me, "My grace is sufficient for thee for my power is made perfect in weakness." It is gladly, therefore, that I rather glory in my weakness that the power of Christ may rest upon me ... for when I am weak then am I strong (2 Corinthians 12: 7–10).

Let us try to see that there may be purpose in the thorns as well as the roses of life. Let us search for the good in the hurts of life, and let us thank God always for everything.

The Power of Display

I WENT TO WALMART THE OTHER DAY TO BUY SOME motor oil and a filter. As I walked down the aisle toward the automotive section I saw this beautiful peanut display and they were on sale. I slowed down, looked them over, and went on about my business, but never stopped thinking about them. I came back by. They were still there — honey-roasted peanuts, my favorite. Well, by this time I could even taste them, so I bought myself a big jar. They put them in a sack for me and I started for the car. When I got in the car I almost had the shakes opening the jar. Well, my hands were dirty, so I just turned the jar up, got me a good mouthful, and oh, how good. They were still in the paper bag when I turned them up. I hope no one thought it was something else.

When I had eaten enough peanuts to calm myself I thought about the power of display. I didn't go to buy peanuts. I wasn't even thinking about peanuts, but that beautiful display out in the open caught my eye. Why do big companies spend billions on advertising and displaying their products? How many people have seen a Red Lobster commercial and said, "Let's go eat seafood tonight?" What about all those liquor commercials? People, perhaps, not even thinking about beer, but there it is in a tub of ice and they watch people drink it. Satan knows and uses the power of display provocatively, skillfully, and deceitfully.

God also knows about the influence of the display. Listen to Moses in Deuteronomy 6:4 beginning as he urges Israel to be faithful, to love God, to keep His commandments. He says,

> impress them on your children, talk about them when you sit at home, when you walk along the road, when you lie down, when you get up, tie them on your hands and bind them on your foreheads. Write them on the doorframes of your houses and on your gates.

Someone doing this today would be called a fanatic. This is exactly what the world is doing. They put it before our children on the radio, on television, the movies, on signboards, while we sleep. Why not put a verse or a good thought on the refrigerator door with a little magnetic holder? Why not a good thought or Bible verse on the door of their room? Why not a gold bracelet for their arm with a message like "Honor thy father and thy mother"? No wonder Jesus said, "For the sons of this world of for their own generation wiser than the sons of light." We have the greatest product in the world, and we hide it under a bushel.

Whose Marriage Ceremony Will I Conduct?

For some years I did not perform a marriage ceremony for anyone who had a living mate because I felt it made me the judge as to which of these had Bible grounds for re-marriage and who did not. This, I later thought, may penalize those who had scriptural grounds, so today if one tells me their mate was unfaithful to them and they were not unfaithful, nor did they cause him or her to be unfaithful, I will conduct that wedding ceremony. I will not attempt to investigate each case. I will leave this in the hands of God. If you hear that I have performed a wedding ceremony for one who has been divorced you will know that they told me their mate was unfaithful to them. If this marriage is not right before God, my doing it will not help. God did not make this rule to be hard but rather to preserve the home and marriage, which is the foundation of society.

The breakdown of the home and marriage is one of the most revealing signs of our times. About half of all marriages will end in divorce. Those divorces will affect just about all the rest of us, and truly we as a society are feeling the effects of the marriage crisis. This, of course. has spilled over into the church. The church is feeling th¢ shockwave from this crisis.

This is not new. Jesus came into a world where divorce and broken homes were a way of life. One Roman was reportedly living with his twenty-second wife, and he was her eighteenth husband. The Jewish men had only to give their wives a bill of divorcement and the marriage was dissolved, so they wanted to know what Jesus thought about it all. They asked him a straightforward question,

> "Is it lawful for a man to put away his wife for every cause?" And Jesus answered and said, "Have ye not read that he who made them from the beginning made them male and female and said for this cause shall a man leave his father and mother and cleave to his wife and the two shall become one flesh, so that they are no more two but one flesh. What therefore God hath joined together let not man put asunder" (Matthew 19:4–6).

Then they raised another question,

> "Why, then, did Moses command to give a bill of divorcement and to put her away?" Jesus answered, "Moses, for your hardness of heart suffered you to put away your wives, but from the beginning it hath not been so. And I say unto you, whosoever shall put away his wife except for fornication and shall marry another committeth adultery and he that marrieth her when she is put away committeth adultery" (Matthew 19:7–9).

Young people. consider this carefully when you choose a

mate. This is not something you can dissolve for mere incompatibility. This is a lifetime commitment that can only be broken by the unfaithfulness of your mate, and if you have caused this unfaithfulness, you are not guiltless. It seems that the disciples understood exactly what Jesus was talking about for they said. "If the case of the man is so with his wife. it is not expedient to marry." If you are not ready for this commitment "till death do you part," then don't marry.

How Will Yours Read?

MANY YEARS AGO TWO BROTHERS WERE DISCUSSING their life goals after Sunday school. The first brother said he wanted to be rich and famous. The second brother said he wanted to follow Christ wherever that led. They both reached their goals. The first brother went on to be rich and had fame. The second brother became a renowned medical missionary and explorer of Africa. His name was David Livingston. When the rich brother died his gravestone read, "Here lies the brother of David Livingston." The one set out to lose himself in the service of others. The other had the biggest house and the finest food and the best clothes and the best transportation. He was the chairman of several boards, but so famous did David become that his rich brother was identified as David Livingston's brother.

There is some similarity in the lesson Jesus taught about the rich man and Lazarus (Luke 16:19). The rich man was clothed in purple and fine linen, faring sumptuously every day. A beggar named Lazarus was laid at his gate full of sores. It came to pass that they both died. Lazarus went to the bosom of Abraham and the rich man to torment. His epitaph might have read, "Here lie the remains of a man before whose gate Lazarus was laid, but he did not give him the crumbs from his table."

The gravestone of the other Lazarus of John 11 might have read, "Here lies Lazarus, the brother of Mary who anointed the Lord with ointment and wiped his feet with her hair" (John 11:2). Though Lazarus and Martha were good, Mary's act became the high water mark of the family. Some will be remembered in infamy, "Here lies Herod, the one who cut off the head of John the Baptist." Here lies Simon the Pharisee, the one whose home Jesus visited—the one who refused to wash his feet or to anoint his head. Here lies Pontius Pilate, the one who washed his hands and turned Jesus over to the mob. Here lies Judas Iscariot, the apostle who betrayed Jesus for thirty pieces of silver.

How might your epitaph read? "Here lies Joe, the husband of his faithful wife, Sarah." Or "Here lies Jane, the wife of her faithful husband, Tom." Or, "Here lies Bill, the son of faithful parents, Jack and Mary." How tragic and wasteful to have been the child of faithful Christian parents or the mate of a faithful wife or husband and live a wicked or indifferent life.

What Do You Make?

A NEW NEIGHBOR WAS WORKING FRUITLESSLY ON HIS mower that had broken down. He could not for the life of him get it to go again. A neighbor suddenly appeared with a chest full of tools and asked, "Can I give you a hand?" In a few minutes, he had the mower cutting beautifully. "What do I owe you?" "Nothing," the neighbor said. "Thank you so much," the new neighbor replied, "and by the way, what do you make with those fine tools?" "Mostly friends" the neighbor smiled. Let me know if I can help you. There are few things in this life that we can make that are more valuable than friends. There is far too much isolation and indifference. In some neighborhoods, there is even hostility. We read of hatred, killing, and fighting, stray bullets hitting innocent people. These are making death and destruction with their tools.

Jesus was the master at making friends. It was said of Him that hands He to went share about burdens, doing touch (Acts 10:38). Jesus used His hands to share burdens, to touch people and heal them, make them well. He fixed more than broken things. He fixed broken lives. He used his ears to listen to the hurts and cries of others. He used his eyes to find those who were in need. He saw them and looked upon them. He used his voice to encourage men, to challenge men as He said to one, "Rise and walk." He even forgave men. "Thy sins which are many are forgiven thee" (Luke 5:23) He used His heart to feel the hurts and wounds of others. "Jesus wept" (John 11:35).

God has blessed us with so many gifts, skills, and talents. What have you made with your gifts, your skills talents, and your fine education besides money? This may be a judgment day question. Some would say they never tore anything down, they never hurt anyone, they never crossed their neighbors' line to trespass. Some would say, "I stayed in my own yard and minded my own business." We need to share our gifts, skills, and talents. We can do all the things that Jesus did. He shared. He helped. He healed. He listened. He taught. He felt. He fed. We don't have to have miraculous power to do these things. Tragically, for so many, these gifts and skills are only for hire. You can't make with your skills and talents a better product than a friend. Wasn't this the message of the "Good Samaritan?" We are all making something. What have you made with your abilities?

The Source of the Problem

A Sunday school teacher was teaching her class of young people the evils of alcohol. She was telling them how alcohol causes deaths on the highway and broken homes. It's the cause of crime and disease and she was urging them never to drink any alcoholic beverages. She noticed one of the children hurriedly sketching something as she was talking to them. She strolled back to see what it was. "Why Johnny," she said, "This looks like a cowboy walking into a saloon." Johnny proudly said, "It is, but it's all right. He's not going to drink nothing. He's just going in to shoot a man." There is a message here for parents, teachers, and the church. The message is this. We must get to the source of the problem with the whole message of Jesus Christ. Young people are confused. Our world says to them, "You can hate but not kill. You can lust but not rape. You can deceive but not lie. You can cheat but not steal. You can have legal drugs but not illegal drugs. Yes, and you can stuff your stomach with all the fatty foods you can pack in as long as you don't drink anything alcoholic with it."

Jesus was the master of teaching men the whole gospel and getting to the source of the problem. He taught men to love God and to love their neighbor and to love themselves. Many of our problems have their source in a lack of self-respect and self-esteem. Jesus taught them to care about God, their neighbor, and themselves. (Matthew 22:37–40) He summed up the law by saying, "As ye would that men should do to you, do ye even so unto them" (Matthew 7:12).

The Pharisees had a narrow one-sided message. They harped on the tithing of mint, anise, and cummin, but they left undone the weightier matters of the law such as mercy and faith. Jesus called them blind guides that strain out the gnat and swallow the camel. They washed carefully the outside of the cup. They gave little heed to the inside of the cup (Matthew 23).

The church today must be careful that she does not harp on the symptoms and ignore the source of sin. Parents and the church today must preach a whole gospel for a whole boy or girl. We must be careful that we do not fall into the pit of the Scribes and the Pharisees.

The great apostle Paul preached a whole gospel. Many times it meant specifying the type of sin that was committed and demanding repentance as in the case of the Corinthians, but he never let their sins drive him into a hobby. Paul told the Ephesian elders at Miletus, "For I have shunned not to declare unto you the whole counsel of God" (Acts 20:27). Paul never left the clear and simple message of Jesus Christ, love for God, love for our fellow man, and love for ourselves. This love will lead us to obey God, to follow Jesus Christ, to care for and help our fellow man, and the self-discipline that will come from loving oneself. All of this will lead to the abundant life.

What's the Rush?

LAST SUNDAY EVENING ABOUT 5:45 A CALL CAME FROM Knoxville, Tennessee, with this message, "We will be home about 10:30. "I want you and mother to meet me at the church building with my grandparents. I want Paw Paw to baptize me." The call came from my granddaughter, Katy, who had been on a mission trip to North Carolina. Katy is one of my ten favorite granddaughters.

Yes, some would ask, "What's the rush? We will do it Monday morning or Tuesday or next week." We're not talking here about taking a bath or washing clothes, nor physical therapy. We're talking here about a new birth (John 3:5), of the forgiveness of past sins (Acts 2:38), of becoming a member in God's family (Galatians 3:26–27), having the maker of the universe as our heavenly father and heaven as our eternal home. We're talking about the greatest goal in life to become like Jesus Christ. Someone has said, "There is no record in the New Testament where anyone who was convicted of sins and desired the new birth ever ate a bite, drank a drop, or slept a wink until they were immersed into Christ." Check it out.

I did not ask Katy what brought her to this urgent conviction. It was not important at the time. I thought perhaps she might have thought, I am teaching others about Jesus and I have not accepted His invitation. It might have been a stirring message she heard on the trip, but most of it came from her faithful parents who took her to God's house before she could crawl or speak and who have shown her Jesus in their lives. This did not happen in a day.

This is urgent, and it is so easy to put off til another day. If you are of age, old enough to understand sin and its consequences, to know what Jesus did for you and what He expects of you, then love and obey Him. This is not for little children. Parents and grandparents pray for your children and grandchildren every day.

That's O.K.

We were in the garden when the phone rang. I rushed to the phone to answer. I was nearly out of breath when I said, "Hello." A man said, "Is Jim there?" I said, "You must have the wrong number." He was so apologetic and kept telling me how sorry he was. I think he had had a little too much cough syrup. His words were slightly slurred, but to put his mind at ease I said, "It's O.K. I've done this myself." Not the cough syrup but dialing the wrong number. That seems to have comforted him.

Walking back to the garden I began to think on what I had said, "It's O.K. because I have done it myself." I'm afraid this is the mindset of this generation. If we've done this or that, it's not so bad. Don't worry about it. It seems to be the thinking behind the polls for the President. With all the allegations the polls are still high. People say even though this is true we don't care. Hey, it's O.K. We all do it, we all lie. Most cheat on their mates. We all try to cover it up, but even if this were true it does not make it right nor wipe out the bitter consequences of our behavior. God will not use polls in the judgment. How much consolation is it for a terminally ill patient to say to another, "It's O.K. I'm dying of that, too."

At the same time, I wanted him to know that we all make mistakes. I wanted him to feel better about his wrong number. This man was very humble, very disturbed that he had bothered me. I was not trying to tell him that it was all right because I had done this, but rather that I dial wrong numbers, too. Had he been defiant saying, "What are you doing at Jim's house," or had he slammed the phone down in my ear, I doubt I would have tried to comfort him. True humility and honesty can bring out the best in the wounded party. It was Jesus who said, "Let him that is without sin cast the first stone." Jesus did not say this to condone adultery but to condemn hypocrisy.

God did not send His son to this world to say, that's O.K., everybody does it, but rather He wanted to show us the seriousness of sin by what it costs to forgive it.

The Noisy Out

WELL, THIS BEING OCTOBER A LOT OF PEOPLE'S attention has turned to baseball. Some of you I am sure are not baseball fans, but a noisy out is when a man gets up and knocks a ball deep into the outfield and the audience stands up and they cheer thinking for sure this is a home run, but it's caught on the warning track and called a noisy out. The batter was all the way to second base thinking he had knocked a home run. The people sit back down, and he walks back to the dugout and takes his place on the bench.

There have been so many men and movements that brought us to our feet with great applause that turned out to be just noisy outs. There were those that got the attention of Jesus and perhaps brought Him to His feet thinking that they would be special, but they turned out to be noisy outs. I think of the rich young ruler who came to Jesus with great excitement wanting to follow Him, one who had kept the law, one who was upright, certainly wanting to know what to do to have eternal life. When Jesus told him the thing that was standing between him and eternal life he went away sorrowful (Matthew 19:16).

In our day there have been political leaders who brought us to our feet. Many thought they had hit a grand slam, but it turned out to be a noisy out. There have been preachers who brought crowds to their feet, even brought them to the front, who turned out to be noisy outs. There have been movements like Communism that brought millions to their feet. It turned out to be a noisy out. There are movements in the church today that are bringing many to their feet with their hands in the air, but it, too, will turn out to be a noisy out.

I think we have to ask the question, "Is my life a hit, a trip home, or a noisy out?" We're all in the game. We all come to the plate. We all hit the ball somewhere, but do we bring others home? Do we contribute to victory?

It Takes More Than
Black-Eyed Peas

Tons of black-eyed peas were consumed on the first day of this year by millions of people. Some washed the peas down who did not even like them. The reason, of course, black-eyed peas are supposed to bring a happy and prosperous new year. I wonder where all of this started. My guess is that some poor mother spent all of the money on Christmas. Then when she opened the pantry she saw one can of black-eyed peas. To get the family excited about this can of black-eyed peas she told them it would bring a happy and prosperous new year. My second guess is that the folks who can black-eyed peas started this tradition, and they will have a prosperous new year.

What we eat and drink for 365 days will have more to do with a good and happy new year than eating black-eyed peas the first day. It could even be related to our prosperity. Good health is such a wonderful blessing. A happy new year may be more related to what we do not eat and drink. The new year might have been better had we fasted and prayed that day. Surely after all we've eaten over the holidays, it would be timely.

We are people who like to believe in luck. If there is any way we can get an edge on the new year whether it's carrying a four-leaf clover or a rabbit's foot or eating black-eyed peas, most will try it. We want some simple easy, good-tasting way to find happiness and prosperity, but really there is no such thing.

The Apostle Paul clearly says that life is not chance but choice. In Galatians 6 he says,

> Be not deceived, God is not mocked for whatsoever a man soweth that shall he also reap. For he that soweth unto his own flesh shall of the flesh reap corruption, but he that soweth unto the spirit shall of the spirit reap eternal life.

The law of the harvest is determined not by what we know but by what we sow.

We might do better to plant those peas, to cultivate them, to pick them. I confess to you that I get black-eyed peas every New Year's Day. My wife may have started all of this. Should I have a good year, however, it won't be because I ate black-eyed peas the first day. It will be because I have sown to the Spirit and because of the wonderful love and grace of God.

A Good Out

THE BATTER HITS THE BALL RIGHT ON THE NOSE. IT looks like it might be a home run, but no, it's caught on the warning track. When he comes back to the dugout, however, all the players greet him with high fives and pats on the back. The reason, of course, is that there was a man on third who scored on the out. This was the game-winning run. This is called a good out.

Life is strange, is it not? The batter before him gets a triple and has to slide into third. This man gets up and flies out, and he becomes the hero. It's true in life that people who get on base do not seem to be as important as those who bring them home, but without the man on third, this batter gets booed. We thank the Lord for those that make us look good and who turn our mistakes into victories.

Someone may think that I am going to conclude that there are good sins if they help others to advance or score, but rather I am going to conclude that there are good sacrifices. This is called a sacrifice fly. It brings a man home, but it will not help the batter's average.

It is also a good out when a great hitter is called on to make a sacrifice bunt to move his teammate to third. Some players do not like to bunt, but they do it for the team.

We need to remember that Jesus laid down, not a sacrifice bunt, but a sacrificed life to move us up, to bring us home. Jesus could have overpowered His enemies at the cross, but His Father asked Him to sacrifice His life so that we might be saved. If you are called on to make a sacrifice bunt, do it. If you have to make an out, make a good one.

Believe It or Not

In Ripley's *Believe it or Not* reports he tells of a man who won the bait and fly casting award. He was the best in the land; yet he never caught a fish. He was known for his great distance and accuracy. You see, he had done most of his casting in his own back yard. He was not really interested in catching fish. He was interested in being the best bait caster. After all, fishing is a little messy. You have to take them off the hook, you know. And it calls for great patience and bearing with the elements.

Believe it or not there are people who have been in the church for forty or fifty years who have never won a soul; yet they pray the finest prayers. They sing with great enthusiasm. They know more Bible verses than most anyone.

My point is this. We have to be very careful that distance and accuracy are not our goals as Christians. This is not a performance in which we play a role on a stage. It is not about records or being better than someone else. Many times fighters before going into the ring simulate a fight. They punch a bag that does not punch back. They are great shadow boxers yet they never won a fight.

God has called us to use our skills, energy, and knowledge to teach, to love, and hopefully, save others. It is said of Andrew when he had been with Christ, "He first findeth his own brother." His goal was sharing this Jesus with someone he loved. The wise man said, "He that winneth souls is wise" (Proverbs 11:30). The amazing growth of the early church was due not to their performance or distance or accuracy but sharing Christ with people with whom they walked.

Hallelujah or Amen?

IN A DENOMINATIONAL CHURCH, A SYNOD WAS ABOUT TO decide whether the local preacher was to remain there or to be moved. While they were considering this, one of the members prayed this prayer,

> Lord, Thou knowest that thy servant, our minister, who now stands before us is to attend the synod. Perhaps the synod will want to station him in some other circuit. If it be thy will to leave him right here amongst us, we'll say, amen, but if it be thy will to send him somewhere else, we shall say, hallelujah!

In its own way, I guess, this is an honest prayer, and it seems to be a reasonable petition. It was brief and to the point, but it seems to bring into focus a reality of life. We do not always get our first choice in life. Many of our prayers will not be hallelujah but amen. Jesus demonstrated this in the Garden of Gethsemane when He prayed that the cup might pass from Him; "Nevertheless," He said, "Not my will but thine be done" (Matthew 26:39). I am sure He would not have said at the conclusion of the prayer, hallelujah, but rather, amen. Maybe this is one of the reasons we close our prayers with amen instead of hallelujah. When Paul prayed about the thorn in the flesh (2 Corinthians 12:7–10), he did not get his first choice, but maybe he got something even better — grace instead of healing — but I am sure it was not a prayer that Paul would say hallelujah but rather, amen. This prayer might be prayed from the sick bed, "Lord, if you see fit to get me well I will say, hallelujah. If not, I will say, amen."

The problem today is that many are looking for a hallelujah religion only. Many might say, "Lord if you can do it my way, at my time, for my pleasure, I will follow you." It is in the amen, "thy will be done" prayer that we often learn and grow. We must learn to pray, "Lord, what is best for you and your cause. What is best for the church, and then consider ourselves." Let's give God some choices in our prayers. Let's remember that He knows best. By the way, I do hope your prayers for me are, "Lord if you see fit to let him stay we will say hallelujah. If he must go we will say, amen." The goal of prayer is to be able to say, "Thy will be done." Hallelujah.

Cotton in His Ears?

Sometime ago I was watching a baseball game on television. I noticed the pitcher had cotton in his ears. My first thought was, bless his heart, he's out there pitching with an ear ache. About that time the announcer gave an explanation for the cotton. He said the cotton was there to cut out all of the distractions. This pitcher wanted to concentrate completely on the man at the plate. He did not want to hear the cheers, the boos nor the experts from the grandstand telling him how to pitch. Since he could not put cotton in the mouths of the fans, he placed the cotton in his own ears. I think we all have to learn this lesson as well.

Jesus used this principle. The Bible says that He set His face steadfastly toward Jerusalem (Luke 9: 15) though it meant His death. He never forgot His mission. He never took His eye off the goal. He said, " must work the works of Him who sent Me while it is day."

Paul used this principle. Paul said in Philippians 3:13,

Brethren, I count not myself yet to have laid hold, but one thing I do; forgetting the things which are behind and stretching for the things which are before, I press on toward the goal of the prize of the high calling of God in Christ Jesus.

We need some of this cotton today. We are letting too many things distract us. We are looking to the right, to the left. We are listening to too many different voices. This only leads to confusion and frustration. We need at times to shut the world out and focus on Him who stands at the gate. The Hebrew writer says,

> ... Let us run with patience the race that is set before us looking to Jesus the author and perfecter of our faith, who for the joy that was set before Him endured the cross despising shame and hath sat down at the right hand of the throne of God (Hebrews 12:2).

Please don't lose your concentration!

Wanted

THIS AD RAN IN THE NEWSPAPER OF ONE OF OUR LARGE cities: WANTED, State Trooper, must be six feet tall with a high school education, can be five-eleven with a college degree, and it might have said, can be five-ten with five years experience.

What does this ad say? One does not have to be so tall, or so strong if one has training, knowledge, and experience.

Here are some other ads that might have run: Preacher wanted: must be six four having a commanding presence in the pulpit. However, he can be six feet if he knows the Bible. If he knows God, five-ten. If he has all of the above and knows and loves and acts like Jesus he can be five six.

Husband Wanted: Must be slim, about six feet two with lots of hair, however, if he is kind, loving, considerate, generous, and unselfish, he can be five-ten, heavy, and bald. P.S. If he remembers special occasions with flowers and presents he can be five-four and wrinkled.

Wanted: A church home. Must be well located, have

easy access, comfortable pews, and be a good preacher. However, if the church is Christ-centered, friendly, loving, active, and involved in reaching the lost I am willing to drive a greater distance and sit on unpadded pews.

Wise people today are looking more at the heart. We've looked too long at the physical appearance. Do you remember when God was looking for a king and Jesse paraded all of his sons and finally David was selected with this explanation: God said, I am not concerned about his height. "Man looketh on the outward appearance; God looketh on the heart" (1 Samuel 14:7).

Could you fill God's desperate want ad for a mother, father, teacher, preacher, elder, deacon, husband, or wife?

Blessed Aids

It's true, we are all getting older, and this is nothing to be ashamed of. The Bible teaches that old age can be a glorious time. The younger are admonished to rise up and honor the hoary head. Moses was not embarrassed to say, "I am a hundred and twenty years old." Some of the greatest Biblical achievements have been accomplished by those who are older. Old age is a witness of God's love and care. David said, "I have been young and now I am old." He was thankful.

We seem to be living in a day that glorifies youth. Many seem to be ashamed and fearful of aging. Billions of dollars are spent today to make us look younger, but Christians must guard against becoming vain.

I had rather have a hearing aid than miss the beautiful sounds of spring. I love to hear the birds sing in the morning. I love the sound of beautiful singing. I love to be able to hear a good sermon. Don't let your vanity cause you to miss the glorious sounds of life.

I had rather wear glasses than miss the glory of one beautiful flower. Aging eyes don't see as well as they once did, but we can be thankful that there are glasses and contacts and even eye surgery that can enable us to see. I was reading the other day and one of the granddaughters crawled up in my lap and with my glasses on I could see more clearly her beautiful eyes and eyelashes. Yes, put your glasses on and lift up your eyes and look on the fields that they are white unto harvest. It is true that you can see without seeing. You can hear without hearing.

I had rather hold onto a walker than sit in a chair all day. As we grow older our strength diminishes. It is amazing how many people have gotten to their feet with the aid of that aluminum walker.

I had rather get out in the sun and chance a few more wrinkles than sit in the shade all day. A lot of the wonderful things that are happening in life are happening in the sun.

I am thankful for that great host of seniors who come to God's house on Lord's Day with their hearing aids, glasses, walkers, pacemakers, colostomies, and with whatever else that makes life a little better as we grow older. Don't let vanity rob you of the golden years. Aging is not for the fainthearted. Remember there was a day when these aids didn't exist.

A Wise Mother

DURING HER SON'S TERM OF OFFICE, THE MOTHER OF President Eisenhower was interviewed on a television talk show. When the host asked. "Aren't you proud of your son?" Mrs. Eisenhower surprised him by saying, "Yes, I am—but which one are you referring to?"

Mothers need the wisdom of Solomon in dealing with the world today. Who else but a mother would give such an answer? This is probably one of the most difficult problems parents have to deal with. Children can be so different. Some of them excel more than others but a mother is equally proud of each one of them. Of course, most mothers never have to deal with a son becoming President of the United States. This answer is a model for all mothers.

Some parents make the tragic mistake that Jacob made in that he loved Joseph and Benjamin more than all rest and demonstrated it through special treatment toward them. It brought envy, jealousy, and hatred within the family.

If someone had asked Jochebed, "Aren't you proud of your child?" She no doubt would have said, "Yes, I am, but which one?" She was the mother of Moses, Aaron, and Miriam. A mother is proud of her children for doing what they can with what they have.

A mother will say, "I am proud of my daughter who is a good mother and homemaker. I am proud of my son who farms this land faithfully and diligently." The mother of Peter might have said, "I am proud of my son who is in prison for his faith and conviction." Had a mother been mentioned in the story of the prodigal son, I am sure she would have said, "I am proud of my son who has returned from the far country. He has grown from his mistakes and can now say "I was wrong, I have sinned, I am sorry." One mother said, "I am proud of my daughter who has made a good home and marriage after several years of struggle."

Who is a wise mother? She must know how to deal with the world in regard to her children. She must be able to seek out those good qualities in each child and praise them. A wise mother knows, loves, and praises all of her children. What a brilliant and loving answer Mrs. Eisenhower gave when she said, "Yes, I am, but which one?" If one should ask God, "Aren't You proud of Your child?" Might He not say, "Yes, I am—but which one?"

The Mountains or Heaven?

I WAS READING ABOUT A PREACHER WHO WAS emotionally drained and physically exhausted. He decided to consult a doctor friend who after a thorough examination found a serious lung problem. He said you need to go to the mountains for at least three weeks. The preacher protested that he had neither the time nor the money for the trip. The doctor took hold of his shoulder and looked right into his eyes and said, "It's either the mountains or heaven." The preacher thought about it for a few minutes then groaned. "Oh, very well then, the mountains."

Do we really believe that heaven is out there? We sing about it: "Heaven Holds All to Me," "Heaven Will Surely be Worth it All," "Beautiful Isle of Somewhere," "Sing to Me of Heaven," and "Won't It be Wonderful There?" But I couldn't seem to find a song about heaven that said, "Take me today." It seems to be the place to go when there is no place else to go. A preacher asked, "All who want to go to heaven raise your hand." All raised their hands except one and the preacher asked him, "Don't you want to go to heaven?" And the man replied, "Oh yes, but I thought you were getting up a trip for today."

Many times Christians carry on at the loss of their loved ones as though there were no tomorrow. I am not talking about tears and grief. That's certainly normal, but Christians must come to realize that death is a part of life and that Jesus came to take away the sting of death and to give us hope so that Paul would say. "That ye sorrow not even as the rest who have no hope." We must not let death make us bitter, angry, fearful, or useless. We must get on with our Christian duties and responsibilities.

Jesus might have been a bit homesick when he said, "Let not your heart be troubled, believe in God believe also in me. In my Father's house are many rooms" (John 14:1–2). It must have been a joyous day for Jesus when Luke reveals in Acts 1:9, "And when he had said these things as they were looking, he was taken up and a cloud received Him out of their sight." The Apostle Paul was caught up into paradise (2 Corinthians 12:4). No wonder he looked forward to being absent from the body to be present with the Lord.

The next time the doctor says, "It's either the mountains or heaven" you can be thankful for Jesus who made this option possible.

Love Suffers Long

A MAN WATCHING HIS FIRST FOOTBALL GAME WITH A friend could not understand why the same team was beating up on each other. They would jump on each other, slap one another on the helmet, grab the face mask, and pull the player up to him, sometimes even knocking him down.

His friend explained to him, "This is the way they show their appreciation for a good tackle or run." The fellow turned slowly to his friend and said, "I for sure wouldn't want to do anything bad down there, if they do this when you do something good, what would they do if you did something bad?"

There is a good point here. People can take a lot of pain and suffering if they know you and God love them. If the other team did this to a player there would be a fifteen-yard penalty and a fight. A child can take the punishment if the child knows you are doing this not out of your anger or frustration but out of love for him or her. A husband or wife can take some criticism if they are sure of your love. Augustine said, "Love me and do what you will." This may be an over-statement, but the principle is true.

Paul at times had to exhort and rebuke, but he always did it in love. Elders, preachers, and teachers have to exhort, rebuke, and correct at times, but it must always be done in love. Paul could take his thorn because he was sure of the love and the purpose of God. Jesus could endure the cross because He, too, was sure of the love of His Father. This love that Paul writes about can take a blow, both of appreciation and discipline. Peter adds to this in 1 Peter 4:8, "Love covers a multitude of sins." (Pain and mistakes).

After all in this country, big, strong, grown men can't kiss each other. If, however, I ever do anything you like I'll just take a hug or a handshake. Thanks.

I Am Disappointed in You

How do you lead children to do the things they should do? We once said, "Do this or I am going to spank you good." Then some said, "Do this or I am going to send you to your room." Then, "Do this or I am going to cry." Then, "Do this and we will go to the park and feed the ducks." One of the new strategies is this, "I am so disappointed in you." As a father, I practiced the first strategy. As a grandfather, these others don't look so bad now. Maybe this is why grandfathers don't need children.

There was a time when we thought a whipping would cure everything. We might have made some children bitter and angry. This is still a good option. However, I believe there is room here to reason with children to bring them to the place you want them to be. Parents, don't forget this. Children must learn there is authority and they must learn obedience sometimes without understanding why.

The children of the nineties can turn these strategies on you. My three-year-old granddaughter, Bailey, told her parents the other day when she didn't get what she wanted,

"I am so disappointed in you." I guess the next thing she will say is, "If you will be good I will take you to the park to feed the ducks. If not, I will have to send you to your room."

There is one thing worse than parents being disappointed in their children. It is children being disappointed in their parents. Children have a right to expect a mother and a father who love each other and to be loved by them. They have a right to expect their parents not only to tell them the right way but to show them the right way with a good example. Nothing can break a child's heart like fussing and fighting parents who eventually separate. It is a terrible thing to break a child's heart.

Surely God must be saying to all the spoiled and selfish parents of this day, "I am so disappointed in you."

Take Care of Yourself

THOSE OF YOU MY AGE MAY REMEMBER THE HIT SONG OF yesteryear which said, "Baby take care of yourself. You belong to me." It was just a pretty tune then. It means much more to me now. The attitude in our world today is this: it's my body, my life, I can do what I want with it. A beer commercial a few years ago said, "You just go around once so get all the gusto you can." I must ask, what about the gusto of those who love and depend on you?

An even stronger appeal than the song is this: take care of yourself. I love and need you. I've seen lately some in my family struggle and grieve through the loss of a wife or husband. It leaves them lost and vulnerable. After listening to my brother and seeing his tears I looked at Jan and said, "Take care of yourself. We love and need you."

We all know there are people who die before their time (life expectancy) who took care of themselves. We know there are diseases. Some are genetic and environmental, but we are told that most die untimely because they did not take care of themselves. Some will be quick to say, but I don't smoke or drink, and that's good, but we are told now that those greasy hamburgers, french fries, and pizza with a lack of exercise and other bad habits can take us before our time. Look at those precious ones who love and depend on you and fold up that recliner and walk.

The final appeal is this: our bodies are the temple of God. You need to take care what you put into it. It is wrong to say, it is my body and I can do what I want with it (1 Corinthians 3:16).

A Rocking Chair Fan

Alabama is my team. I really like the Tide. I always watch them when they play on television and listen most of the time when they are on the radio, but I've only been to the stadium a couple of times in my life. I think we got there late and left early. I wear no logo on my jacket or cap, or bumper. I would never lift up a stick with a box of Tide and a roll of toilet paper on it to say "Roll Tide." I don't want people to think I'm a fanatic. I don't write letters of encouragement when the team is winning or losing. I do criticize a little bit when they are losing but mostly to my wife. I never send them any money. I don't pray for them. Well, maybe once or twice this year. It seems like it was the Houston game and Ole Miss. Where was I when they needed me? I've never encouraged a young person to go to Alabama, and I've never been to a pep rally. Mostly, I just rock and watch. Wonder why none of my children went to the University of Alabama.

It reminded me of the way many feel about the church. Some really believe in the church, if they went anywhere they would go to the church of Christ, they watch the church on television and listen to the radio, and once in a great while they attend worship. They get here late and leave early. They don't talk about the church to anyone. They wouldn't dare lift up the cross. They don't want anyone to think they are a fanatic. They have never been influential in bringing anyone to Christ. They never offer any encouragement when things are going well but quite often criticize when things are bad. They seldom ever give any money, nor do they participate in the activities of the church. Mostly, they just rock and watch.

Here is what a real fan looks like. He or she buys a season ticket, goes to all the games, he cheers to the top of his voice. He is there no matter what the weather — rain, snow, thunderstorm. He wears the name on his cap, on his jacket, and on his bumper. And he has pictures of the "Bear" in his house. He encourages the coach, and he knows all of the players. He gets to the game early, and he stays until it's over. They talk about Alabama football everywhere they go. They will get in your eye if you run down Alabama. They do more than rock and watch. Guess where their children go to school?

These real fans remind me of the early Christians, their zeal, devotion, and fervor for Christ and His church. When I, a rocking chair fan, die and a real fan dies I wonder who will be missed the most. What about you and the church? Are you just a rocking chair fan?

Won't They Ever Forget?

Don't you know that the Japanese have dreaded December 7, for about fifty-three years? They have to relive their infamous attack on Pearl Harbor. The world will remember old movies will be shown, and old soldiers will tear up when they remember. There was a twenty-fifth anniversary and three years ago a fiftieth anniversary. The warriors are old men now, and many of them are already dead.

Many other things happened on December 7, 1941. Some were born. Many died. Others were married. There may have been other tragedies that day, but it is this one the world remembers. In about two hours on that December morning America lost eight battleships. six major airfields. almost every plane, and 2,400 men. Our world would be changed from then on.

One thing we learned is this. We have to live with our choices and deeds in life. Not only did they suffer great consequences in losing the war. but each December 7, there is the memory of their attack on Pearl Harbor, without a declaration of war. What other nation in the world but America would have put Pearl Harbor behind them after the war and helped the Japanese become a super-industrial giant? Pearl Harbor says something about America as well. Her ability to rally, to fight for the right, and even to forgive.

To answer the question. "Will they ever forget?" Yes. The next anniversary will be the seventy-fifth. Virtually every soldier will be dead by then. Maybe it will be bad to forget because then it may happen again. There were bad experiences God wanted Israel to remember. Their bondage in Egypt for me, but how quickly they forgot those hard times and that God brought them out "Remember thou wast a slave in the land of Egypt" (Deuteronomy 5:15). We tend to forget the good things as well. Sadly, the book of Exodus opens by saying. "There arose a new king over Egypt which knew not Joseph" (Exodus 1:8). Jesus said, "This do in remembrance of me" (1 Corinthians 11:24). This we must never forget.

Unmaking My Day

A YOUNG LADY TWENTY-FIVE OR SO AND I GOT ON THE elevator at Helen Keller Hospital. As we were passing the time of day she asked me what floor, and I said "The third." She said, "That's where I'm going." When the door opened to the third floor I smiled and motioned for her to go ahead. "Oh no," She said, "You go first." I said to myself as I walked down the hall, "Do I look that old?" You know, I wanted to tell her that I still run and jump, and have my original teeth. I play tennis at times with my grandson, and once in a while, I climb a tree to shake pecans.

There are people who know how to unmake your day. Even though she did it with the best intentions in the world and really it didn't matter to me, but can I tell you young ladies something? Unless the old man is in a wheelchair or holding a walker or has no teeth and you are pretty sure he couldn't climb a tree, you go first. Some men are very sensitive, you know.

I think I told you about the lady who told Jan one Sunday how pretty she looked and then added, "You don't look like yourself" One has to think about that for a while before one says thank you, but knowing the sister, we knew she meant well.

My point is this. We must use a little tact and diplomacy along with our politeness. Unlike those mentioned above there are those people who try to hurt others with compliments, like the lady who said, "I like that pretty dress. I saw one just like it at the 5 and 10-cent store."

Jesus endured this Himself when He was standing before Pilate. Pilate said, "Behold your king" (John 19:14). If you didn't know Pilate you would think this was a compliment, but it was meant to hurt. Again in John 19:4, Pilate said, "I find no fault in Him." It sounds like a compliment but in reality, he wanted to wash his hands of Jesus.

Don't wrap your sarcasm in the paper of kindness or politeness.

The Perfect Hiding Place

It is hard today to hide things where they cannot be found. There are metal detectors and even dogs that are trained to sniff out various scents. Some places would expose our treasure to dampness, others perhaps to fire, and others to theft. The greatest treasure in this whole world is the word of God. There has never been a book like it. Through the ages there have been those who have hated and despised it and would destroy it. David seems to have found the perfect hiding place for the Word of God. "Thy word have I hid in my heart . . . " (Psalm 119:11).

Yet, we tend to forget as we grow older every word of the verse. I remember an elderly sister trying to recall a verse. She couldn't put it all together. She, however, had hidden that verse in her life, in her conduct and disposition. She lived that verse on love and kindness that she couldn't quite quote. Hiding the word in our deeds may be the most effective and the most lasting place to hide God's word. There have been places and are still somewhere Bibles are not allowed. Men and women are punished for having them in their possession. The only word we may have someday is the word we have stored in our hearts and in our conduct. Neither prison, blindness nor confiscation can keep it from us.

The hidden word has many values. David says it keeps us from sinning against God (verse 11). It also keeps us from sinning against our fellow man and from many foolish mistakes. Hid in our hearts, it is a light to our pathway (verse 105). This will keep us from stumbling in the dark. David says it brings us understanding. "Through thy precepts I get understanding; therefore I hate every false way" (verse 104).

How do we store it? We must love it. David said, "Oh, how love I thy law. It is my meditation all the day" (verse 97). Then, too, we must study it. "Study to show thyself approved unto God" (2 Timothy 2:15). We must also live it and apply it.

How much of this treasure have you hidden in your heart and in your conduct? Who then has hidden the most of God's word? The one who looks the most like Jesus, for Jesus is the Word. (John 1:14).

Before and After

One of the most persuasive arguments for a product is the before and after effects. You see this a lot on television and in the newspaper. It's probably most used with weight loss, and this diet pill will do for you. Sometimes they show a man without hair, then how he looks after he has his new hairpiece. Many times there is a noticeable difference. Some are worse.

What kind of evidence are we of the power of the word of God? Paul in 1 Timothy 1: 12–13 talked about his before and after with Jesus " ... though I was before a blasphemer and a persecutor and injurious; howbeit I obtained mercy because I did it ignorantly and in unbelief." Paul's change was so dramatic that many people could not believe it. This causes people to ask questions and to investigate. It gave Paul an opportunity to tell men what changed his life. (Acts 26) David could say, "Before I was afflicted I went astray but now have I kept thy word." David is appealing to his before and after. Mark tells of the demoniac who lived in the tombs. Men had to bind him with fetters and chains, but he would break them into pieces. He was riddled with self-inflicted cuts from the stones. But after he had been with Jesus, he was clothed in his right mind, sitting at the feet of Jesus. (Mark 5:1–20).

God has a picture of each of us before and after. Is he pleased with your progress? Are you a good recommendation for Christ? Peter talked about men and women who have become worse than they were when they started and what a terrible fate. He said, "It is like the dog turning to his own vomit again and the sow that was washed wallowing in the mire" (2 Peter 2:20–22).

Remember this is the ultimate and final evidence in a Christian's life — not how much Bible you know, nor how many church services you attend, nor how many prayers you pray, but rather are you like Jesus? It was said of the early church, "They took knowledge of them that they had been with Jesus" (Acts 4:13).

Ninety-five and Looking Ahead

AFTER A STANDING OVATION IN A PACKED HOUSE, SIR Willam Hurlock, ninety-five years of age, made his way to the podium. His voice was firm and clear as he spoke. It was the voice of love and optimism. Among the outstanding things he had to say was this:

> I am still at work with my hands to the plow and my face to the future. The shadows of evening lengthen about but morning is in my heart. The testimony I bear is this: that the castle of enchantment is not yet behind me. It is before me still and daily I catch glimpses of its embattle-ments and towers. The best of life is always further on. Its real lure is hidden from my eyes somewhere behind the hills of time.

We have learned that people have a much better chance to live to be old when they have something to look forward to, work to do, and some reason to get up in the morning.

People seem to live longer who are looking ahead rather than behind.

My dad will be 85 in May of this year. He is doing full-time work as a minister. He preaches twice every Sunday. He does funerals, weddings, he studies, he visits, he baptizes. The folks there refuse to let him retire, but then he doesn't want to retire.

Certainly for the Christian, the best of life is always ahead. The wise man said, "Say not thou what is the cause that the former days were better than these? for thou dost not inquire wisely concerning this" (Ecclesiastes 7:10). The Psalmist said, "They shall still bring forth fruit in old age" (Psalms 92:14). God warns, "That if a man beget a hundred children and then live many years so that the days of each year be many and his soul be not filled with good ..... I say, that an untimely birth is better than he" (Ecclesiastes 6:3).

It is true for the Christian that the castle of enchantment is before us. "In my father's house are many rooms" (John 14:2).

On Singing a Solo

Did you ever hear a great chorus sing? Their voices blend so beautifully together. You have the sopranos, the altos, tenors, and basses. You are moved and inspired by their beautiful singing. Yet what you may not know is that each of these singers had to sing a solo before they could sing in the chorus. The director wanted to know what part each could sing and the quality of their voices. The director wanted to know the range of their voices.

Someone has well said, "In the chorus of life it's easy to fake the words, but someday each of us will have to sing a solo before God." There is no way we can get into that great heavenly chorus without God judging our song individually.

I think we all need to be reminded that we can hide out on the back row of the chorus in this life and perhaps no one here will even notice, but remember you and I must sing our solo before God. Last Sunday morning the singing was good, but did you sing? Last Sunday morning the contribution was good. It was $7,500.00, but what did you give? There were more than four hundred deeds and acts of kindness and love, but how many were you involved with? Many seem to think that we are going to be judged as a church. God is going to take us all in a group, but it is not so.

It's true, it's easy to fake singing or giving or praying or working in a large church, but God's ear is listening to each individual heart. I am not saying here that you have to have a beautiful voice or give the most or pray the longest, but you are required to do the best you can. There will be a great chorus over there. The apostle John saw a great chorus of those victorious over the beast, "And they were singing the song of Moses and the song of the lamb" (Revelation 2:3).

Paul says in 2 Corinthians 5:10, "For we must all appear before the judgment seat of Christ that each one may receive the things done in his body according that he hath done, whether it be good or bad." Are you ready to sing your solo, and how will you fare alone?

A Cure for Worry?

A New York merchant came in to work looking haggard and with bloodshot eyes. His boss asked, "What's the trouble?" "Can't sleep for worrying" he said. His boss said, "Try counting sheep. It will really help." He came in the next day looking worse than ever. "What's wrong now," asked the boss. "Well, I counted 50,000 sheep, then I sheared them and made up 50,000 overcoats. Then came the real problem that kept me awake the rest of the night. I could not find 50,000 linings." This may be closer to the truth than we realize. Some can't count sheep without making overcoats without linings.

Worry takes a great toll on the body. Charles Mayo says worry affects the circulation, the heart, the blood pressure, the whole nervous system, and the glands. Worry can cause ulcers and there is probably no part of the body that it does not adversely affect.

Too often we worry about nothing. A patient at a mental hospital stood with his ear to the wall listening intently. "Shhh!" he told the nurse who walked into the room. The nurse quickly pressed his ear to the wall and said, "I do not hear anything." "No" whispered the patient, "It's been like this all day." He was worried that there was nothing to worry about. How true this is. We look and listen for things that never happen.

Someone has well said, "When you have finished your day, go to bed, go to sleep, God is awake." Another said, "Worry is like a rocking chair. It gives you something to do but gets you nowhere." There are two days you should never worry about — yesterday and tomorrow. This would kill most of the worry. One man said, "Worry is like shoveling smoke." Another said, "I am so poor I can't afford to worry." It is true the devil would have us climb mountains that are not there and cross rivers that do not exist. Worry is a form of atheism because it lacks trust in God.

Jesus taught us the folly of worry. "Who by worrying can add an inch to his height?" He asked us to look at nature, the lilies of the field, the helpless sparrows. Without worry God takes care of them. Jesus says when we worry we are like the Gentiles, people without faith. Then he lovingly tells us He knows what we need, then promises us that when we seek His Kingdom and His Righteousness all these things will be added unto us. (Read Matthew 6) Counting sheep is not a cure for worry; being like a sheep in the Good Shepherd's fold is the cure.

Forgiveness Is Not Yours to Give

A FATHER SENT HIS SON FAR AWAY TO WORK IN THE Peace Corps. He loved his son more than anything. While he was there he did so much good helping the needy, teaching the ignorant, and binding up the wounds of the sick. The father was so proud of his son.

While he was there a gang of jealous, hateful men took him and shamefully killed him. The father's heart was broken. He had lost his only son, a son who had given his life to help, heal, and save.

Later the men were found and brought to trial. The judge hearing the case forgave the men and turned them loose. They were of a prominent tribe and the judge wanted to appease them. But the father said to the judge, "It was not yours to forgive. I am the wounded party. Forgiveness lies with me."

There are too many today offering forgiveness and salvation arbitrarily on their own terms, but it is not theirs to offer. It is God who has been wounded. It is His Son who was crucified. Who are we to set the terms of pardon? You talk about judgmental. Here is a case in point.

Jesus, after rising from the dead, gave His terms of pardon, "Go into all the world and preach the gospel to every creature. He that believeth and is baptized shall be saved" (Mark 16:16). He had already told Nicodemus, "Except a man be born of water and the spirit he cannot enter the kingdom of heaven" (John 3:5). His chosen apostles were authorized to remit sin. After Peter's bold sermon on Pentecost (Acts 2:37), the crowd said, "What shall we do?" Peter said, "Repent and be baptized in the name of Jesus for the remission of your sins." Saul was told by Ananias, "Arise and be baptized and wash away thy sins" (Acts 22:16). The Bible emphasizes there is more than something to feel. There is something to do. This includes loving God and our neighbor.

Well, some might say, we thought more would respond if we made it simple and convenient. It is not up to the church to decide the terms of the pardon. Only God can pardon us, and only His terms are valid.

Beauty Is Not Enough

You can't help noticing and admiring the beautiful flowering Bradford pear trees. They are breathtaking, but if you planted them looking for fruit you will be disappointed. These blossoms only tum to leaves, but their beauty is so shortlived. Beauty is for a day, but loveliness is forever.

Perhaps these justify their existence just by being beautiful, but we are not one of these. God did not put us here for decoration. Adam and Eve were told to be fruitful and multiply. God wanted them to produce and to care for the garden and to reproduce their own kind. I feel sure they did not lie around and pose as though they were in a picture frame. I am sure their days were filled with fruitful activity, and what joy would life be if we had nothing to do and nothing to become?

Have we in the church lost this God-given exhortation? Have we come to think that we are in the church for decoration, or that there is empty space in the garden and we are to fill it with trees and foliage? No, we too are to produce and reproduce our own kind. Jesus asked in the parable of Luke

13:6 when he saw a fruitless tree, "Why doeth it cumber the ground? Cut it down." Jesus is saying we must justify our right to exist. Jesus saw a tree as a parasite taking and giving nothing back. Three years had passed, and it had produced nothing. God does not do things in haste. He is patient and kind, but there comes a time when the tree must be removed.

Let us learn from the flowering pear tree that beauty may thrill us but it will not feed us. When the day is over we must have nourishment. Jesus was hungry and needed food (Matthew 21:18). He was not looking for decoration or scenery but life-giving nourishment. He is looking for the same thing in us.

Beauty, then, is not enough. Our world is preoccupied with beauty. We have lost sight of spiritual nourishment. On the day of judgment, you will not be asked, "Were you pretty, but were you fruitful?"

We Need Both Ends of the Pencil

Jan tells the grandchildren that the only spanking she ever got in school was for biting the eraser off her pencil. This came from her father who was filling in for the regular teacher. This seems like such a trivial thing today, but back then a pencil was a prized possession because these were hard times and one did not bite off one's eraser. It worked. She never bit off another eraser and never had another spanking. I sure wish I could say that.

What was she thinking about to do such a thing? Well it didn't affect the writing part, and I guess she didn't plan to make any mistakes. Most likely it was soft and the only part of the pencil that looked edible. Remember these were hard times.

I guess her father wanted her to know that in life you need both ends of the pencil. With one end we make our mark in life, and there are times we need the other end to remove that mark. Perhaps the lesson is that you don't alter things in life that have purpose just because you can.

Most of us know now why they put erasers on pencils.

We can't all be like Pilate who said, "What I have written, I have written." Pilate had said, "Jesus of Nazareth, King of the Jews." If only he had said this out of conviction instead of derision. It is true we have erased some things that were right, and we have refused to erase some things that were wrong.

God knew we would need both ends of the pencil as it were. He sent His Son to teach. His instructions were written down. God knew that mankind was lost and in need of forgiveness. Jesus gave His life to erase our sins if only we would believe in Him, confess our sins, and turn from them, then be born again into His family. Don't bite off the head that can erase your past and make possible the forgiveness of your sins.

Jesus wept over Jerusalem because He knew they were going to bite off the only hope they had. And look how they have suffered. I pray that we do not repeat Jerusalem's mistake.

Surrender, The Best Choice

Do you remember those Iraqi soldiers coming out of their trenches bowing and kissing the hands of the American soldiers? They had been used by their leaders as cannon fodder to slow the American troops. They were afraid. They were hungry. They were dirty and bewildered. They surrendered unconditionally. You remember they came by the tens, then the hundreds, and then the thousands. They came as it were from the graves to life, sunshine, and freedom.

But sometimes in war surrender can be taken for advancement so there had to be terms of surrender. The Allies dropped thousands of leaflets. The terms were plain, simple, and in their own language. The message said, "Lay your weapons down. Put your hands over your head with this white paper in hand." This is exactly what they did. They had either a white piece of paper or a white piece of cloth. White is usually a symbol of purity, but in this case, it was a symbol of defeat and humility.

God has offered us life, pardon, and freedom in plain and simple language, but the only way to it is unconditional surrender. Some do not accept this offer because they, like many of the Iraqi soldiers, are threatened and intimidated by others who want to fight and defy to the end. Still others do not come because they want to negotiate their freedom. Others do not surrender because they are ignorant of the terms. Still others are afraid it's too good to be true. They stay in their graves. They ask, "Who would offer such a thing to a people like us?" Others feel they can fight their way out or think their way out or slip away to freedom, but most of these die violently on the day of confrontation.

These came for the same reason we must come to Christ. We are wrong in what we have done. Our position is hopeless. We are spiritually hungry, dirty, and bewildered. We like they are fighting against Him who wants peace, who wants to save our lives and souls. We like they are overpowered. God could easily crush us. Yet He sent His only Son to ask us to lay our weapons down, to give up the sinful life, to surrender our wills and He would pardon us and make us His own children by a new birth (John 3:5).

Surrender is not only the best choice. It is ultimately our only choice. This is what Saul of Tarsus did on the road to Damascus. He surrendered to Jesus and said, "Lord, what do you want me to do?" You need to lay your weapons down today and surrender to Jesus.

Satan's Solution

MANY YEARS AGO A MAJOR AMERICAN COMPANY OPENED an assembly plant in Panama. Very quickly, however, they ran into trouble keeping the employees working. The assembly workers had little to buy in Panama and bartered for the things they needed. This left them with more cash than they could spend. So, periodically they quit working until they could spend the cash they already had made. Well, there were many attempts to solve this problem. One said, "Pay them less; hold some of their payback." Others wanted to move the plant. Finally, someone came up with the suggestion that they give all of their employees a Sears catalog. This worked beautifully. It wasn't long until they were all in debt and had to work every hour of every day to pay for their pretties.

Is not this Satan's solution to so obligate us with things that we have neither time nor money left for God? I am very concerned today that many young people, single and married, are so obligated that there is little left to give to the Lord.

Never have there been so many beautiful things to buy in the marketplace. Never has it been so easy to buy them. Some things can be bought without interest. Other things can be bought now and you don't start paying for one year. Then, too, there is a little plastic card that works magic. Consumer debt is at an all-time high running into the billions. One can end up giving God the crumbs from the table. This, too, can leave us no time at all for rest or worship. It has caused family problems and even divorce. Some have ended up in bankruptcy court. Never has there been a time when we needed to practice restraint and self-discipline as we do today. We must learn to say no.

Satan offered Jesus his catalog in the wilderness: beautiful things to eat, to wear, to have, to own. Jesus said no. He quoted to him from God's catalog, "Man shall not live by bread alone" (Matthew 4) Jesus said again, "Take heed and beware of covetousness for a man's life consisteth not in the abundance of the things which he possesseth" (Luke 12:15).

Satan does not say to us, curse God and die; rather try this delicious fruit. You will like it. Young people, put God generously in your budget. He will bless you.

Shaping or Finishing?

I was looking at the handle of a fingernail file the other day and on one side it said "shaping" and the other side said "finishing." Every woman knows that one side is for rough nails, cutting them down, and the other side is for finishing them up. One side is coarse, and the other side is very fine. Carpenters are aware of this same principle. They use coarse sandpaper when they are shaping a piece of wood and when it's finally shaped they use fine paper to give it a good even smooth texture.

God, too, has a shaping and finishing file. Just as we have a purpose in mind with a file, so does God. God is trying to shape us into vessels of honor and usefulness. He may start with the shaping abrasive side to form us, then he turns to the finishing side to perfect us. We mustn't fight the file. God has something beautiful in mind for your life. Does the fingernail flinch or move from side to side when you are trying to shape it into something beautiful? Does a fine piece of wood move about when the master carpenter is shaping it into a beautiful piece of furniture? Job said, "Shall we receive good at the hand of God and not correction?" (Job 2:10) David said, "It is good for me that I have been afflicted (or filed) that I might learn thy statutes" (Psalm 119:71). "Behold I have refined thee ... in the furnace of affliction." "My son, despise not the chastening of the Lord" (Hebrews 12:5). Then he says, "Afterward it yieldeth the peaceable fruit of righteousness" (Hebrews 12:11).

The side of the file that God uses may, to some degree, be up to us. Paul in writing to the Corinthians said in 1 Corinthians 4:21, "What will ye that I come unto you with a rod or in love in the spirit of gentleness?" Parents are aware of this in dealing with their children. Children who are at times rebellious and defiant call for the abrasive side, but as they learn and mature we can use the finishing side. Let us pray that God will use the side it takes to make us into something useful and to get us home at last.

The Shelf Life

A while back I bought a five-dollar tube of the best caulking compound I could find. It promised to do it all-pliable, withstand heat and cold and would last a lifetime. I used some of it and was pleased with it. I put the cap back on it and put it on the shelf. A few weeks later I needed it again and it had hardened. I lost the rest of the expensive tube. Sometime later I needed an epoxy to fix something. I turned the package around and read the fine print. After reading all of its wonderful qualities I saw something that really caught my eye. This product had a shelf life of twenty years which meant to me you don't have to use it up all at once and it will be there when you need it.

So many Christians have a short shelf life. They have a lot of wonderful qualities provided you use them up at one time. Many Christians like glues and epoxies tend to harden over the years and become useless. The tube still looks good. It still sits on the shelf, but when you need it most you find out it is set in its ways. Sometimes the tube cracks and all of the contents ooze out-all of the love, the kindness, the goodness, and the generosity.

Sometimes you can get a little more out of a tube by surgery. They usually go bad up around the neck of the tube so I make a puncture in the middle of the tube. This is a terribly messy way to get the contents out of a tube or a Christian, but these are desperate times.

For many of these products as well as Christians had they been used up and passed on it might have been said, "What a great contribution" but they ended up dried up, hardened, cold and useless.

There are those in the church who keep on giving year in and year out. They are still pliable and useful. Oh, they are not as fast as they once were and they can't always remember which end to squeeze, but they are still loving, kind, generous and I thank God for each one of them. Could the Psalmist have been talking about the shelf life when he said, "His leaf also shall not wither and whatsoever he doeth shall prosper" (Psalm 1:3) or "They shall still bring forth fruit in old age ... to show that the Lord is upright" (Psalm 92:14–15).

Before You Glue

Did you ever work with any PVC pipe? It is some kind of heavy plastic pipe that many plumbers are going to today. It has several advantages. It is light. It will not rust. It bends, and it is easily joined together. There is to me one disadvantage. When you apply the glue the pipe is set for life in less than a minute. I ought to know. I have a collection of the prettiest little Ls and Ss you could see.

I am almost paranoid about gluing now. I measure it several times, and then I have trouble putting the glue to it because of my collection, and I realize it's final. There are many things in life that you can re-do, but not much where glue is involved.

I think of marriage as a permanent glue. Jesus said, "What therefore God has joined together let not man put asunder" (Matthew 19:6). The word joined means a type of glue. Thus God has permanently joined these two together for life until death does them part. I wish more were paranoid about this union, thus to say, "Is this the right one? Am I prepared to live with him or her for the rest of my life? Is this the father or mother I want for my children?" Remember with the pipe when one has not measured properly both joints are ruined and cannot be used again.

Thankfully, God has made an exception to this rule- unfaithfulness on the part of one. (Matthew 19:6) Don't forget there is damage even to the innocent party. I am not writing this article for the one's who have already used the glue. Some know the pain and loss of breaking the joints apart, but rather to those who have not yet applied the glue.

There are some who are trying to put the joints together without glue —living together without marriage, but these pipes leak and won't hold the pressure, and they are acts of fornication in the eyes of God.

I do not know how we can get this across to our children and our grandchildren, but you might go buy a piece of this pipe and let them glue it together and then tell them to take it apart. This may give meaning to the words: "What God hath joined together."

The Miracle Spaghetti

AFTER CHRISTMAS WITH THE DELICIOUS HAM, TURKEY, dressing, and cranberry sauce, I thought some spaghetti would be nice. Jan made up a big pot of spaghetti and meat-balls. It was actually noodles and meatballs. We ate spaghetti for days, and every time it seemed to grow bigger. I know it must swell when you warm it up. That's why I called it miracle spaghetti. I would ask, "What's for supper?" She would say, "How about spaghetti, you wanna spaghetti, you gotta spaghetti." She speaks a little Italian. Then I came up with a great idea of putting it in a fancy bowl and melting cheese over the top and having all the kids over. I figured it would take about twenty-seven to clean it up. We never got them altogether.

This reminded me of the manna in the wilderness. It came with the dew every morning. However, they were to get just enough to last that day. Those who tried to hoard it found it spoiled the next morning. This is where Jan made her mistake. She tried to make enough for the whole winter.

I know this wasn't miracle spaghetti, but I declare, it

looked bigger every time we warmed it up. This reminded me of God's gifts. You do not use up the sun that warms us. It just keeps shining even when the clouds are over it. The moon does not stop its reflective glory. We take enormous amounts of water from our rivers and lakes, but they just keep on giving us more water from the good rain that falls on the earth. How is it that the ground, year after year and generation after generation, keeps giving us food? The air we breathe is not used up with all the billions that breathe it. This is no mere accident, this is a miracle set in motion by God in the creation.

But even greater are the spiritual blessings. We cannot exhaust the love of God. In spite of our weaknesses and failures, God still loves us. God's love is patient. He waited in the days of Noah while the ark was preparing for men to change. The prodigal did not exhaust the love of God. When he repented God met him with open arms. His forgiveness cannot be exhausted as long as His children can repent. The Psalmist says in Psalm 86:5, "Thou Lord art good and ready to forgive and plenteous in mercy unto all them that call upon Thee."

No wonder Jeremiah says in Lamentations 3:23 speaking of the mercies of God, "They are new every morning. Great is thy faithfulness."

Author Unknown

I OFTEN READ AN INSPIRATIONAL POEM OR ARTICLE ONLY to find at the conclusion, "Author unknown." We like to know who wrote this or who said that. We like to know something of the heart and the life of the person who wrote. Writing is such a hard and difficult thing, and someone who does well deserves credit. Why is the author unknown? Sometimes the author is so concerned about the message, he forgets about his name. Many times it is the carelessness of the copier who simply fails to identify the author, and the next person who picks this up has to say, "Author unknown." Then it spreads further and further. Sometimes it is malicious. People do not want to identify the author or give him or her credit. Some put no name at all thinking that it will be assumed that they wrote the article.

It is dishonest for us to put into print the writings of another person with our name attached to it. Many preachers preach week after week the material and lessons of other men without any acknowledgment. Let it be remembered that Jacob fooled Isaac, but he did not fool God. Old Isaac said to Jacob his son, "The voice is the voice of Jacob but the hands are the hands of Esau." How true this is today. Well might we say, "The voice is the voice of Jacob, but the message is the messagae of Esau?" I am sure, however, that all these unknown authors are thankful that their work is being used, that men are reading it and are better for having read it, and certainly they know that God knows who the author is. I guess in the final analysis this is all that really matters for God will give credit. He will give credit for the good, and He will give credit in the way of punishment for all of the evil that is put into print. Many would like to say on judgment day "Author unknown."

Jesus was a master at giving credit to others. Quite often he would quote a prophet as in Matthew 15:7: "Well did Isaiah prophesy of you, saying." He constantly gave credit to His Father. In John 14:7 He said, "My Father is greater than I." Peter gave credit to Paul, "Even as our beloved brother, Paul, also according to the wisdom given to him wrote unto you" (2 Peter 3:15). What else would you expect from these great men? They loved each other and they loved the cause and they were honest and generous men who had been with Jesus.

Paul says render to all their dues. "Tribute to whom tribute is due ... honor to whom honor" (Romans 13: 7). We are too quick to blame and too slow to give credit.

Optimism or Innocence?

WHILE PLOWING IN THE GARDEN THE OTHER DAY I turned up several earthworms which delighted my grandson. He decided he would get something to put them in so we could go fishing. He ran to the house and was gone for a few minutes. Then I looked up and saw him dragging a 30-gallon plastic tub that we use to put leaves and the like in.

I was a little outdone and said pessimistically, "Son, no, no, you will never fill that big tub with worms. What you need is a little can." Well, his face fell and he decided, well, if you can't fill a big tub like this, why bother?

When I thought about my words as I continued to make my rounds with the plow, I thought to myself that this was not the right way to handle that. Let him believe he can fill it. Let him try. If he fills it, fine. If not, he will learn that you might need to fill the small cans first, or, perhaps, there are not as many worms in life as I thought.

Have we, as adults, those who know everything, squashed the dreams and optimism of our youth by saying,

137

"Oh, you need a tiny little can for your dreams. You can't fill that big tub."

David was told by his wise brothers, "You are but a youth. You can't fight Goliath." In essence, "Who do you think you are?" He was a youth with faith in God and one who had not lost his sense of righteous indignation, and he filled the tub with the head of Goliath.

Remember when men were told, "It is impossible to fly? The horse and buggy will never be replaced? Men will never go into space." Remember Joseph was called the dreamer by his brothers, but the dreamer ended up saving his people from starvation.

You can become a preacher, a song leader, an elder, a deacon, or a Bible school teacher. We can reach the world with the Gospel. Bring a tub. You will need it.

With the Door Wide Open

A LITTLE WREN FLEW INTO OUR UTILITY ROOM THE other day, and when I found her she was almost exhausted. With the door wide open, the door she came through, she was beating herself to death at a closed window. When I tried to help her she flew to another closed window. Finally, I caught her. She pecked my hand, but I set her free.

We ask, why could she not find the door she came through? It seems she was completely disoriented. This led to panic, and she was preoccupied with the light from the closed window. Birds get their bearings from the open sky.

How true this is of man who has left the God who made him. Why can't they get out of sin? Because sin disorients man. He loses his sense of direction of right and wrong. Jesus said of the prodigal son, "When he came to himself" implying that sin distorts man's senses. The prodigal tried other ways to save himself like feeding the pigs, but it was a closed window.

This is true of children who have flown into a walled room. They so often fight the ones who try so hard to free them. It is true of our lost world. A loving God sends His only son to free us, and we nail Him to a cross. He tried to tell them and us, I am come that ye might have abundant life. I have come to release you, to free you from the bondage of sin.

One thing we should learn, both young and old, is you don't go into every room just because the door is open. We find in life so many open doors inviting us to come in. This room was not made for a wren. There are rooms not made for man. They are places of danger, enslavement, and ruin. You must fly on lest you become like this little bird.

Some look at the little wren and say, "How stupid," when they themselves are banging their heads against a barred window when the door to God's freedom, forgiveness, and peace is wide open.

Hanging On

A storm hit our pecan tree about a year ago and twisted one of the limbs leaving it hanging straight down by just a few threads it seemed. This year I was shocked when I looked up and saw the limb with green leaves on it. Someone had said, "You need to get that limb down before it falls on somebody."

But it's hard to cut a limb that is green and still productive. In life, we try to save anything that has life in it. They are putting severed hands back on now. We can save a tooth that has been knocked out. With CPR many times a heart that has stopped can be started again. We hate to give up as long as there is hope.

Jesus taught us to be slow with the ax. He taught that love is very patient. In the parable of the fig tree in Luke 13:6, the vinedresser has come three years seeking fruit and finding none. He said, "Cut it down. Why doth it cumber the ground?" But the vineyard keeper begs for one more year. He says, "I will dig about it and fertilize it and if it bears fruit thenceforth; well, but if not, thou shalt cut it down." We need patience with each other. Many have been cut down prematurely. If he waited three years for a tree to produce, we should be careful about cutting a green limb off.

So many have been twisted by the storms of life, yet they are still hanging on, and still productive. Paul seems to be writing about this very thing in 1 Corinthians 4:8, "We are pressed on every side; yet not straightened, perplexed yet not unto despair; persecuted yet not forsaken; smitten down yet not destroyed." Paul seems to answer the question "How can we hang on?" He gives the reasons in the rest of the chapter. He saw the outward man decaying but the inward man renewed daily. He saw afflictions as light and for the moment and building strength in us. He was not distracted by the things seen because he kept his mind on the things that are not seen. And in chapter 5:1 he says, "We have an eternal house. One not made with hands."

The difference, perhaps in success and failure, saved and lost, is one's determination to hang on.

You're Not Alone

These words were on the wall in one of my doctor's office. You know, you move from the first waiting room to the second waiting room, and there is usually time to fret, think, pray, and read the wall posters. This one caught my eye. In bold letters it said, "You're not alone." Then listed below were many of the diseases we have in common in this world.

I know this is there to bring a little comfort. You are not the only one with this disease. There are many others. I guess this needs to be said. There are some who suppose they are being singled out for suffering and pain and perhaps untimely death. Poor old Elijah needed this sign. He thought I am the only one left, the only one to suffer this rejection when all the time I was doing Your will and work. He was told, "There are seven thousand like you who have not bowed the knee to Baal." There are others who have suffered for their faith and conviction and many to come.

We must remember that God has never promised us freedom from disease and suffering. He did not choose to isolate us in a germ-free environment. We must mix and mingle to save the sick and dying. The same genes that bring us wisdom, strength, and beauty, also carry genes of Alzheimer's, cancer, and heart disease.

If God had offered freedom from disease to all righteous people, then churches would be filled for the wrong reasons. It would be, me and now rather than others and tomorrow.

Jesus did not die to save the body but rather the soul. One must remember some of the most righteous men and women who ever lived suffered. I think of Job, the apostle Paul, and even God's only Son, and many, many since then. Health and longevity, great as they are, are not the goals of the Christian life, but rather faithfulness, submission, duty, and service. In short, becoming like Jesus.

It is true, you are not alone. You are not the only one. For many years now I have been preaching and trying to get it into my thick skull that this life is not so much about what happens to us, but what happens in us and through us.

In 2,000 years it won't really matter how we felt but how we live and for whom we live.

Please Count Your Words

While writing a couple of articles recently for *POWER FOR TODAY* they specified no more than two hundred words and advised, "Please count each word." It tends to make one very selective and very careful of the words chosen. This might be good advice for all of us. Please count your words. This process also makes us weigh our words. Count them and weigh them as though you were writing them at a dollar a word. Count them and weigh them as though you were going to have to eat them from a tape recorder. Perhaps nowhere is there more waste and extravagance and even corruption than in our conversations.

Why did they ask me to limit my words to two hundred? Space is one reason, but beyond this, they hope it will produce greater quality. They want you to cut the chaff and give them bread. They want you to take three sentences and make one. In short, they want people to read it and get something from it.

It seems that God was counting His words when He gave us the Bible. The creation story is told in one chapter or thirty-one verses, and the fall of man in twenty verses, each with a reading time of two or three minutes. One of the greatest and most loved chapters in all of the Bible is the twenty-third Psalm, and it has but six verses and a reading time of twenty seconds. It has brought hope, consolation, and peace to millions.

Jesus summed up all the Old Testament commands in two commandments. "Thou shalt love the Lord thy God with all thy heart, soul and mind" and "Thou shalt love thy neighbor as thyself" (Matthew 22:38–39). The prodigal son said to be the greatest short story ever written, has twenty-one verses and a reading time of less than two minutes. Peter, in one verse, tells us what to do to have our past sins forgiven (Acts 2:38). Paul's address at Athens is reputed to be one of the greatest ever given. It has ten verses and a reading time of thirty seconds.

The wise man says, "Be not rash with thy mouth" (Ecclesiastes 5:2). Again he says, "The fool's voice is known by a multitude of words." And let us all remember, "By thy words shalt thou be justified and by thy words shalt thou be condemned" (Matthew 12:37). The wise man also said, "A word fitly spoken is like apples of gold in settings of silver" (Proverbs 25:11). Please count your words.

"I Like Your Cap"

"ARE YOU A DODGE MAN?" "No," I SAID, "I JUST LIKE their caps." The cap had a ram logo with Dodge written across it. My brother, Jay, gave it to me. Now, he is a Dodge man. He wears a Dodge cap and sings their praises. I just like the color—tan and red, and good quality. I just wear it on special occasions. It's not a work cap.

A cap can be a real benefit, almost a necessity. It keeps the harsh sun out of your eyes. It is great when you are having a bad hair day. They are wonderful to cover those bald spots from the blistering sun.

It reminded me of how our Christianity could be like this cap. Something we wear to cover our bald spots (our sins). Then at times to hide our uncontrollable hair and to cover our eyes from the light of the sun (Son), but is it no more than a convenience to us? Is Christianity like this cap, something we picked up at home or something someone gave us? Is it a name or a logo in whom we really believe? Do we drive the product, and are we driven by it?

Could this be one of the problems we are facing today in

the church? We wear the name but do we even "talk the talk" much less "walk the walk." Could it be that we are wearing a logo (name) we have not experienced, nor is there trusting faith, but rather a cap we picked up with an adjustable band-one size fits all band—one size fits all?

What eventually happens to this free cap? Well, it gets old, colors fade, and it is tossed in the closet or maybe in the garbage. After all, someone else gives us a new cap that's white and red or purple and gold. After all, this was not really my cap, my belief, I just liked the colors.

Somehow we have to lead our children to a faith of their own. Our cap—our faith will not sustain them through the hostile environment of this world. I like your cross, "Are you a Christian?" "No, but my folks are. I just like the gold cross and chain."

When Excuses Become Lies

SOMEONE HAS SAID AN EXCUSE IS A LIE WRAPPED IN tissue paper with a ribbon on it. Excuses are lies when they intend to deceive. Many excuses are half-truths. You remember Aaron and the calf of gold he made. When Moses questioned him he said, "You know how these people are. They gave me their gold, and I put it in the fire, and out came this calf." Part was true but he tried to deceive, trying to cover himself (Exodus 32:24).

Do we deceive when missing worship with a sickness, then up and out on Sunday afternoon or at work the first thing Monday morning?

Do we deceive when we say, "I could not attend worship because I was staying with my sick child?" Then we leave her for other reasons and are gone longer than a worship period.

Do we deceive when we say we could not get out because of the weather, then go to other places in the same kind of weather or worse?

Do we deceive when we say, "I came to worship and no

one spoke to me?" So, I'm not going back, knowing that we rushed out and spoke to no one. Do we stop buying groceries, gasoline, or medicine because no one spoke to us?

Do we deceive when we say, "I'm not going back to worship because there are hypocrites?" Our country is filled with hypocrites. Some sell our secrets to the enemy. Others are in high places, but you haven't left the country yet, because you realize this is inevitable.

Do we deceive on the first day of the week when we say we are giving as we have prospered and as we have purposed in our hearts, knowing that we spent far more on worldly things?

If excuses are intended to deceive then they are lies. We must remember that the Apostle John put liars in the same category as murderers, fornicators, and idolaters, and the punishment is identical. "Their part shall be in the lake that burneth with fire and brimstone" (Revelation 21:8).

"Man looks on the outward appearance; God looks on the heart" (1 Samuel 16:7).

The One that Got Away

IF YOU'VE EVER BEEN AROUND FISHERMEN VERY MUCH you have heard them tell about the one that got away. It was usually a big one, but I'm going to tell you about a little one that got away after he was caught and put in a plastic bag. It seems that one of our beloved elders, Woody Walker, who is so often thinking about others, decided to take his maid a mess of fresh fish. So he took them out of the live well, put them in a bag, and put them in the back seat floor of his new Jeep wagon. The fish being alive and fresh flopped until they got out of the bag. One of them flopped under the front scat. This is the one that got away. Woody gathered the others up and gave them to his faithful maid. Days later Woody began to smell something but could not find where the odor was coming from. Losing a fish you know is not like losing a silver dime or golden ring. After the fish ripened for about two weeks, he found it.

There are some lessons to be learned here. Some would say one should not transport fish in one's new car or one should count one's fish when taking them out of the bag, or, perhaps, one's fish should not be so fresh.

But to me there are some much deeper lessons. There is a powerful lesson here on influence. Woody removed the fish but its influence lingers in his car. Is this not true of bad men and women? You may bury their body but their influence lingers. Hitler has been dead for about fifty years, his remains burned, but the odor lingers in our world. Jesus Christ died almost two thousand years ago, but He left the sweetest fragrance in our world. It was said of Able, "He being dead yet speaketh." What fragrance will you leave?

Could it not be said that this sinful world has the stench of corruption because we, too, have flopped away from our Creator and our intended purpose into a dark narrow place to rot and waste away? How bad was the odor you asked? There is a rumor out there that Woody picked up a hitch-hiker who rode with him a block and said he believed he would walk the rest of the way. Woody asked him where he was going and he said to Memphis. Perhaps the truth of the matter is that the odor in his car is a witness for good — for one who went about doing good for others without thinking about the cost. How many people do you know who would put fresh fish in their new car because they wanted someone special to have them? I love this man.

Also by Cypress Publications

Always Near: Listening for Lessons from God by Bill Bagents

The Christian Life: Chapters for Bible Teachers by Ed Gallagher

Easing Life's Hurts by Jack Wilhelm and Bill Bagents

Getting My Heart Right With God by Bill Bagents

Jesus the Christ: Chapters for Bible Teachers by Ed Gallagher

The Magnitude of God: Exploring the Divine by Brian Poe

Rescue: God and Sin in the Old Testament by John F. Wakefield

Revisiting Life's Oases: Soul-Soothing Stories by Bill Bagents

That All May Go Well: Why Christians Prosper, Why They Don't, and Why It Doesn't Matter by Coy Roper

Visions of Restoration: The History of Churches of Christ by John Young

Welcoming God's Word: Reading with Head and Heart by Bill Bagents

Women in the Shadows by Betty Hamblen

CYPRESS
PUBLICATIONS

An Imprint of Heritage Christian University Press

To see full catalog of Heritage Christian University Press
and its imprint Cypress Publications, visit
www.hcu.edu/publications

www.ingramcontent.com/pod-product-compliance
Lightning Source LLC
Chambersburg PA
CBHW031527120626
46545CB00005B/2037